JUMP

AND THE NET WILL

APPEAR

JUMP

AND THE NET WILL

APPEAR

DISCOVERING THE ART OF ACHIEVEMENT
AND THE RHYTHM OF SUCCESS

ROBIN CROW
Foreword by BRIAN TRACY

NEW WORLD LIBRARY
NOVATO, CALIFORNIA

New World Library
14 Pamaron Way
Novato, CA 94949

Cover design by Mary Beth Salmon
Type design by Mary Ann Casler
Typography by Tona Pearce Myers

Library of Congress Cataloging-in-Publication Data

Jump and the net will appear : discovering the art of achievement and rhythm of success / by Robin Crow.
   p.   cm.
Includes bibliographical references (p. 149) and index.
  ISBN 1-57731-230-9 (hard cover : alk. paper)
  1. Crow, Robin. 2. Guitarists—United States—Biography. 3. Sound recording executives and producers—United States—Biography. 4. Success. I. Title.
  ML419.C76 A3 2002
  781.64'092—dc21   2002005978

First printing, September 2002
ISBN 1-57731-230-9 (hardcover)
ISBN 1-57731-247-3 (paperback)
Printed in Canada on acid-free, partially recycled paper
Distributed to the trade by Publishers Group West

10   9   8   7   6   5   4   3   2   1

To my four wonderful children, Savannah, Nakota, Joseph, and Andrew, and to my wife, Nancy, for quietly teaching me the most important lesson of all — the deeper path of raising a family

CONTENTS

ACKNOWLEDGMENTS

During the year and a half I was writing this book there was always a whirlwind of activity on all sides. While recording a new album, overseeing the completion of two more studios at Dark Horse Recording, and embarking on a new album with Jon Anderson, I had the privilege of crossing paths with literally hundreds of people who have made my life a richer experience and who influenced this book. I am deeply grateful to...

• My parents, J. and Patty Kilpatrick, for your amazing support, even when you suspected I was jumping off a diving board into a pool with no water.

• My family at large: Laura, John, and Frank Runge; Beth, Joel, Sara, and Mark Maybee; and Louise and Virgil LeQuire. And to Doc, Ruby, and Emil Crow... in loving memory.

• The success magnets — Jana Stanfield, Tim Bays, and Mike Rayburn: Your support, encouragement, and advice have lifted me up when I could not stand on my own strength. According to my dad we'll always be "the starving motivators." And a special thanks to Mike for using the phrase "*Jump...and the net will appear*" in one of our conversations. I wrote it down and here's the book!

• My staff at Dark Horse: Ed Simonton, Todd Wells, Shelley Bright, and Davina Sprinkle — for your tireless hours to keep this place running twenty-four seven.

• Ted Judy for making Dark Horse into a true work of art. You really are a Renaissance Man, perhaps the best carpenter in the known universe, and, more important, part of our family here.

• All the craftsmen and work crews who helped me realize the dream and creation of the *new* Dark Horse Recording, especially Brent Seaton, Tom Blackburn, Stan Justice, Bobby and Jackie DeLoach, and Bill (Hatchet Head) Story. We're not done yet, just taking a short break.

• Marc, Munro, Marjorie, Mary Ann, Georgia, Tona and the rest of my new family at New World Library — with special thanks to my genius editor, Jason Gardner.

• Vic, Dan, and everyone at Nightingale Conant.

• David Dunham — thanks for being the first to catch the vision of *Jump and the Net Will Appear,* and Andy Andrews and Robert Smith — thanks for introducing me to David!

• My mentor, P. J. Hickey, for taking me under his wing with great advice and counsel.

• Joshua, Geraldine, and Dr. Slack — thanks for supporting me with your time, energy, resources, and debates for twenty years now.

• Bill and Jan Horn, for sticking with me through thick and thin.

• My friends with whom I've shared many hours in wondrous conversations exchanging philosophies — Kevin Teeple, Doug Allen, Bill Bellet, Jennie Adam, Faith Gorski, Becky Robbins, Jon and Jane Anderson.

• Floyd Boggs; Ryan Smith at Shure Microphone; and Chuck, Dick, and everyone at the Krispy Kreme Corporation.

• Clarke Schleicher, Brent King, and Rocky Schnaars, for working tireless hours engineering my latest album, and to Ken Mansfield, Chris Fischer, Elisa Elders, Beth Lewis, and Dan Lacy for career counsel.

• Greg Godek for introducing me to my literary agent, Joe Durepos, and Joe for introducing me to New World Library.

• And to all who have recorded at Dark Horse during the last eight years...you have enriched my life by allowing me to be a part of your music and by giving me the pleasure of spending time with you.

FOREWORD

Robin Crow is an amazing success story. Starting with practically no money, he has achieved seemingly unachievable goals through hard work and by learning and practicing the principles he shares with you in this book. Robin presents what he has learned in a wonderfully accessible way — through his real-life stories — that will help you accomplish those goals of your own that always seem just out of reach. No abstract theories here!

As a veteran musician and entrepreneur, Robin has embraced the science of personal achievement and used these strategies to turn his life around. This book will show you how Robin went from struggling musician to successful businessman, author, and speaker. And, more important, you will learn how to rise above the obstacles that may be holding you back from achieving *your* dreams.

Just seven years ago, this talented guitar player was completely broke and trying to find a way to support his wife and four children. But with passion and commitment, Robin has forged ahead not only to achieve incredible business success but to create a wonderful family life as well.

Robin is a role model for anyone who aspires to blend their talents and goals with the success strategies and inspiration needed to achieve them! Now, with the help of the methods he shares in his book, he is living a life most people only imagine.

This is the kind of book that will inspire you and motivate you to achieve greater things than you ever thought possible. Read this book from cover to cover and then follow the advice in the title: *Jump and the Net Will Appear!*

Brian Tracy
Author of *Maximum Achievement*

PREFACE

When Robin Crow asked me to write the preface for his book *Jump and the Net Will Appear,* I leaped at the chance. Why? Because I've seen his remarkable transformation close up, and can only hope you'll take time to learn from his journey as well. Interestingly enough, this book began working its magic before it was even published. I was on a cross-country plane trip with manuscript in hand, intending to write this preface, when the man sitting next to me asked to read a few pages. Thirty minutes later, I wrestled the book from his grasp as he spilled out his story. "It's incredible! This book is exactly what I needed to read at this moment in my life. I have been tortured about whether to start my own business or stay in the safe world of accounting. The answer is now clear to me." What an affirmation!

It seems like almost yesterday that I was riding with Robin in his "concert truck" — an old Ryder, loaded down, with balding tires and no air conditioning to chase away the Tennessee summer swelter. Robin spoke of his dreams and goals and how he planned to achieve them. Now, realize this was a single guy with a good heart. a national recording artist, but broke — living in a one-bedroom apartment and spinning his wheels. However, the more he shared his dreams, the clearer it became to me that his study of human behavior was about to pay off. Robin had studied success patterns through mentors such as Brian Tracy, Napoleon Hill, Stephen Covey, Tony Robbins, and so many more. Now it was his turn.

His formula — have faith, set goals, then jump! — started to show results immediately with incredible, positive life changes. Each goal he achieved was replaced by higher, more aggressive goals. Of course, with all my CEO wisdom, I began to caution him to "start playing in safe now." Cheerfully thanking me, while ignoring my advice, Robin would charge off to the next challenge!

Now, you ask, did any of these dreams come true? Let's see: within a few short years, I attended his wedding, held his newborns, listened to his new CDs, and stood on the top floor of a spectacular, world-class, Robin Crow–designed recording studio. *Jump and the Net Will Appear* is loaded with such inspirational true life stories.

This book is already changing the lives of people who have read it. I will be encouraging the 14,000 people who work in my company's restaurants to read this special work. I encourage you to do the same.

Philip J. Hickey Jr.
President/CEO
Long Horn Steak Houses / RARE Hospitality, Inc.

INTRODUCTION

Making our dreams come true can be hard. Sometimes it's not until we find ourselves completely desperate, with everything on the line, that we're willing to do something about it. Sometimes it comes down to taking that leap of faith and going for broke. Sometimes we just have to *jump...*

Creating an extraordinary life doesn't happen in a day. It takes persistence and perseverance. It takes self-control and discipline. It's sometimes painful. But mostly it takes making that first decision to change. And you can. How do I know? Because I've done it! But not before I earned my Ph.D. in the school of hard knocks. For the first twenty years of my adult life I stumbled and fumbled my way into a career in the music business. I toured year in and year out, traveling more than a million miles on U.S. highways. I thought I was on the road to success. I thought I was following the path to achieving the American dream, only to find out, as I turned forty, that I was lost and clueless.

Since the first time I picked up a guitar, I have lived, breathed, and slept music. I love everything about the music business: writing new songs, being in all-night recording sessions, giving interviews, rehearsing. I love wandering through strange cities, all-night bus rides, making friends, hanging out backstage, waiting for the show to begin...and then the payoff: performing my heart out in concert!

Unlike those performers on vhi's *Behind the Music,* I don't have a sensational story of rags to riches, then alcohol and drug abuse, then at last a magnificent comeback. Unless you're a hardcore fan of eclectic guitar music or you've stumbled onto one of my performances while channel surfing, you've probably never heard of me. That's okay, because I've discovered something far more valuable than being this month's superstar. I've discovered how to attain true success in life. And that's why I wrote this book.

Every one of us dreams of a life rich with happiness, health, and prosperity. We all believe deep inside that we have unique talents to offer, that we are here for a purpose — to make a difference and to benefit others. But often this vision of fulfillment — and our zest for life — begins to fade as we get caught up in the frustrations of day-to-day survival. Living in the real world challenges our faith and our hope of achieving the quality of life we've dreamed of. Slowly our dreams crumble into so many pieces that we eventually give up trying to put them back together again.

But we *can* break these mental chains and find freedom! We all have the ability to lift our thoughts, to take charge of our lives and shape our circumstances. And that's what *Jump and the Net Will Appear* is about — resisting fear when it tries to make a home in our hearts. It's about finding strength during tough times, learning how to create an extraordinary life, and using our God-given abilities to turn our dreams into reality. Discovering this simple truth — that God gave us the ability to shape our fates — offers us a tremendous source of strength. It empowers us to experience life at its fullest, to take charge of our destiny, to bring forth our unique offerings to the world to make a difference.

Although I had an outwardly exciting career as a concert performer and recording artist, I could never really keep things together. I was like an airplane sailing down the runway at 115 miles per hour when I needed to go 120 to lift off and fly. I realized that it didn't matter if the runway was a hundred miles long; without that extra burst of power I was never going to become airborne. Finally, when my back was up against the wall and I had reached my threshold for anguish, I began studying the habits of successful people — not because it sounded like an exciting idea, but because it had become painfully obvious that I simply didn't know it all.

To my delight I was amazed at what I discovered. As simple as it might sound, I began to realize that to be successful we must first become success conscious. It's about developing new habits. Of course, I haven't achieved perfection or eternal bliss. I didn't become smarter than Bill Gates or better looking than Tom Cruise. But after twenty-five years of learning lessons the hard way, I've learned that an excellent life is within my grasp. I'm living proof that even a guy like me, who failed English and never went to college — who didn't possess the natural musical skills of my friends and who was broke at forty — can pull himself up and turn things around.

Once I started studying how to be successful I realized I had to ask myself some questions that had gotten buried under the weight of my day-to-day struggle to survive as a musician:

What are my core values and beliefs?

How can I have a deeper and richer life experience?

Can I have a successful career, wealth, and a fulfilling family life?

Is it possible to achieve these things while remaining spiritually balanced?

What is my real definition of success?

Discovering the answers to these questions has completely turned my life around. But it took me a long time to learn some simple lessons. Once and for all I stopped listening to the naysay-ers. I was through being influenced by other people's limiting beliefs. I was armed with a solid vision of achieving a life of abun-dance for myself and my family. This sense of purpose compelled me to find ways to overcome obstacles that used to stop me cold in my tracks. By setting goals — emotional, physical, and financial — I began heading down a path that has brought about a life of abundance greater than anything I could have imagined just five years ago.

Perhaps many of the changes I'm talking about are subjective, but the massive change in my finances is not. Almost overnight I began amassing wealth beyond what I had ever dreamed of. And while climbing the mountain of financial independence, I have been having the time of my life! Starting with just $2,000, I turned my small home recording studio on my ten-acre farm in Franklin, Tennessee, into a multimillion-dollar, world-class studio complex called Dark Horse Recording. It has become a haven for some of the biggest pop and country stars in the world, such as Wynonna, Dolly Parton, Neil Diamond, Jewel, Faith Hill, and Amy Grant, to record, as well as a place for me to work on my own music. I'm now the owner of a successful business, performing for larger audiences than ever before and planning other adventures that will take me far beyond what I thought possible.

All this happened for me because I learned how to tap into hidden potential and strength I didn't even know I had. This awakening has brought about positive change for my entire family. As a husband and a father of four, raising a family has been a path of spiritual growth with amazing challenges and blessings. A positive attitude and a belief in unlimited possibilities have brought us overwhelming happiness and led us down a road to deeper fulfillment. Like a seed that has brought forth new life, my life has become an exciting journey full of wondrous possibilities.

As its title — *Jump and the Net Will Appear* — suggests, this book is about taking risks and learning to embrace the unknown. My motto has always been "A ship is safe in the harbor, but that's not what ships are built for." In the following chapters I will share my stories with you. Some are humorous. Some are extraordinary. All are personal accounts of persistence, determination, and growth that I hope will inspire you. This book is a wake-up call for anyone on a quest for a deeper and more meaningful life, to anyone who doesn't ever want to settle for less than the best life has to offer. So don't be afraid to follow your heart. If you're willing to jump, your net will appear.

CHAPTER ONE

LEAP □F FAITH

When I was a child, I dreamed I could fly like the wind
Time after time after time,
I would spread my wings and pretend
As the years went by, I settled for less
But the time has come to put it to the test
It takes a leap of faith, when the moment of truth arrives
It takes a leap of faith, to truly believe I will fly
I know the further I climb, the further I may fall
But this time I'm risking it all

— **"Leap of Faith," Robin Crow and Karen Staley**

I t was August 14, 1992, one of the biggest days of my career. In two hours I would be giving interviews to local news crews at a record store in Dayton, Ohio, where my newest CD, *Electric Cinema,* was selling like hotcakes. That night I was scheduled to perform in front of thousands of people under the stars at the Dayton amphitheater along with the pop-jazz group Spyro Gyra. Meanwhile, my truck had broken down just forty miles away from my destination, and I was flat on my back staring up at a dirty engine, pretending to be an auto mechanic. Once again things weren't going as planned.

Electric Cinema had just been released on RCA and was in every store in the United States. I was on fire to make a name for myself, and take my place as a national recording artist once and for all. After all, it was about time! For the last twenty years I had toured endlessly. I had spent every waking moment clawing and scraping my way to this point. It seemed like there wasn't a single two-bit dive I hadn't performed in. There wasn't one lonely highway I hadn't been broken down on. There wasn't a truck stop parking lot I hadn't slept in.

But, forever the optimist, I just knew this was the year everything was going to fall into place. Even though I was thirty-eight years old, even though I was still broke, even though I was living like a vagabond, even though I was still sleeping in my converted Ryder truck — camper in front, gear in the rear — I knew that now my time had come. My name was on the marquee along with Spyro Gyra, and I was part of the reason that people were laying down their money.

For two months I had been going nonstop, opening up for acts like Peter Frampton and Cheap Trick. I had been on national TV half a dozen times, and I had a song that was making its way up the New Adult Contemporary radio charts. But tonight was extra special. Because John Manus, the enterprising owner of the CD Connection chain, began playing *Electric Cinema* over the store speakers, a spark had turned into a runaway wildfire of sales in Dayton. I was almost famous!

Having driven about 450 miles from the previous night's concert in Missouri, my guitar tech, stage manager, and I were grabbing our typical four hours of sleep while parked in an interstate rest stop, just like we had a thousand times before. At 10:30 A.M. the summer heat was already steaming up our six-by-eight-foot living space. Covered in sweat, we began discussing where we might find a shower before my 1 P.M. in-store appearance. With less than an hour's drive ahead I leisurely fired up the truck and headed down the entrance ramp toward the interstate. Then ka-blewee! Steam started rushing out every crack in the hood, even into the cab. This was major!

I quickly pulled over to the side of the road, where it didn't take long to figure out that I had blown the radiator hose. Believe me, I'd been waylaid a hundred times before by truck failures, but today this was not acceptable. There was no time to lose. I had no choice but to crawl under the truck and do *something* to fix the problem. So in 90-degree heat I slid under the engine with my box of tools and began unscrewing things. Then with one last wrong turn of my wrench the entire radiator full of fluid gushed out, completely drenching me in green antifreeze. I closed my eyes. "I'm thirty-eight," I thought. "I'm a national RCA recording artist on tour, yet in twenty years *nothing has changed!*"

Why was I still living hand-to-mouth?

Why was I unable to justify spending money on a nice hotel? Was it because I couldn't come up with the extra $100, or was it because I didn't understand what it meant to become success conscious?

Was I somehow unknowingly sabotaging myself?

I was working hard but obviously not "working smart." Often I would make $3,000 a night to perform a 90-minute concert. Yet

I was stuck on what seemed to be an endless treadmill in a career that demands complete effort at all times to keep up. Show business can be very deceiving. I've known many artists in the national spotlight, with songs on the Billboard charts, who would be out on the street in a month if they quit touring because of the enormous overhead required to keep a national career going. That's how it was for me: lawyers, accountants, road crew, trucks, sound systems, light systems, managers, agents, and my own office and assistant all kept me in the poor house.

By the way, I did make it to CD Connection, which was packed with fans and news crews. I was late, hot, and sweaty. My hair looked like someone had poured glue on it. But I played my songs, smiled, shook lots of hands, and lived up to the show biz tradition that "the show must go on." Then I headed for the concert venue, took a shower in my dressing room, and proceeded to give an enthusiastic but mediocre performance in front of thousands. It could have been an excellent performance if I had been working smart.

Does this sound glamorous? Fulfilling? Successful?

Was I living the American dream, or was God just having fun giving me a *taste,* but never a full meal, of what I had worked so hard for? After twenty years I had achieved this fractured version of my dream career, but in reality it was closer to that high school nightmare I used to have where I'd be performing, only to look down and discover I was in my underwear. My life seemed like a puzzle, and I had managed to only put a part of it together correctly. When I looked at the picture of my life as a whole, it wasn't complete; it didn't make sense. I didn't feel successful as a recording artist or, really, as a human being.

LEAP OF FAITH

> **Being completely honest with yourself is a crucial step in bringing about lasting change.**
>
> **Don't let another day go by where the gap broadens between you and your dreams.**

Once upon a time I based everything on this belief: If I could play the guitar faster and louder than anyone else, I would be successful and happy. So I became completely obsessed with my goal. I concentrated twenty-four/seven on becoming the biggest, baddest, leanest, meanest guitarist to hit the concert stage. My goal was simple: to rule the Billboard charts and play the biggest and most prestigious venues in the world — forever! The great thing about being young is that logic doesn't stop you from doing what you want. Basking in my ignorance I set off on my course to fame and fortune. And out of sheer persistence I tasted a bit of it along the way. Sure, I was happy for a moment here and there. There's nothing like getting a standing ovation or hearing your music being played on the radio. But I never *did* manage to rule the pop charts. I was forever touring, all right, but my stops weren't at Madison Square Garden, five-star restaurants, and the Ritz. I was playing at college student centers, eating at Taco Bell, and sleeping in my truck.

Yes, I was following my dream, but as I climbed the ladder of success I never took the time to notice that it was leaning against the wrong wall.

I didn't know how to balance my life.

I didn't know how to get ahead financially.

I didn't know how to manage my time.

I didn't have a plan that made sense.

In short, I didn't understand the principles of success that I will be talking about in this book. Most important, I didn't understand that it was my responsibility to redesign my relationship with myself before I could begin reshaping my world.

CHANGING MY MIND

Can people really change? I did! I changed my core beliefs about myself. I changed the way I perceived the world around me. I changed my thoughts and attitude. I went from someone who believed that the universe was somehow conspiring to keep me down to someone who now believes the world is conspiring to help me succeed.

I remember when I first started to change. I was running out of steam. I had worked diligently all my life. I didn't smoke or drink or take drugs. I went to church on Sundays. I helped little old ladies across the street! But I was mentally and emotionally exhausted. When I looked in the mirror I would ask, "Is this the best I'm ever going to do?" "Is this as good as I'm ever going to feel?" "Is this as happy as I'm ever going to be?"

Then to add insult to injury, RCA dropped me. I was thirty-nine years old, and I didn't know any other way to earn money except writing and recording records or trucking across the country with my road crew and tons of gear, giving concerts. The problem was, after performing almost two thousand concerts and releasing seven albums, I still could never get ahead. And things were getting tougher instead of easier. When is the last time you saw people getting excited over a middle-aged musical newcomer? I kept thinking of that album by Jethro Tull, *Too Old to Rock 'n'*

Roll: Too Young to Die. Was this going to be how it all ended? Was I doomed to become a pathetic has-been guitar player who couldn't cut it in the real world?

So the fact that I changed wasn't because I was fearless or brave. I simply had no choice. I was up against the wall. My despair was so great that I *had* to take some kind of stand. I knew if I didn't the pain would become unbearable.

**Hitting bottom can be the best motivator
for making positive change.**

**Knowing you *should* move forward and
committing that you *will* move forward makes
all the difference.**

I did two things that completely changed my life. First, I began seeking advice from people who were successful not only in their careers but also personally — people who seemed happy and fulfilled. I began reading everything I could get my hands on, studying the habits of some of the world's most successful people. Like a detective searching for clues, I began searching for practical ways to make my life work.

*Instead of spinning the dials of life hoping for
a lucky break, as if you were playing a slot machine,
you must instead study and emulate those who
have already done what you want
to do and achieved the results you want to achieve.*

— Brian Tracy

I was searching for basic principles to help me take my life to a higher level of achievement and personal satisfaction — universal laws that our creator set in motion to help us succeed in life. So for the next five years I listened to thousands of hours of audiotapes, and I began attending seminars on personal development and achievement. I committed myself to changing my attitude in the belief that it would, in fact, change my world. And it did!

The second thing I did was to *take action.* All the knowledge in the world means nothing if you don't put it to good use. It was obvious I had to venture into unknown territory. So I jumped! Taking a giant leap of faith, I stepped completely out of my comfort zone and started my own business — half out of excitement and half out of fear.

But wait a minute! Robin Crow a businessman? No way! It was all I could do to balance my checkbook. This change was painful. My entire identity was wrapped up in being an artist who lived and breathed music. As far as I was concerned, running a business was not something I could do. But slowly I began to stack one small success on top of another, until pretty soon my identity began to expand beyond musician to successful business owner. It started becoming clear to me that I could have achieved far more success as a recording artist if I had only understood and applied the principles I was now learning. But there was no looking back. Now I was putting everything I had into turning my home recording studio into a world-class business.

Then I made the most amazing discovery. By learning to take responsibility I began to notice consistent and predictable patterns that gave me the edge I needed to succeed at whatever I put my mind to. What's even more amazing is the speed at which I was able to accomplish these things. These discoveries began to completely change my mind-set. All these years I had been carrying negative preconceptions about business because I had been afraid of it. Once I discovered it was a game I could win, I began to embrace it. It was as if I had been given a new lease on life. Once again I became excited about waking each morning. And you know what? Every aspect of my life changed: my relationship with my children, my marriage, and, of course, my finances. In fact, in just three years my life went from *nightmare* to millionaire! Getting there did involve some risks, but the rewards have been more than worth it.

TAKING RISKS

You say you're not a risk taker?

Oh, yes you are! Think about it. Every morning when you start your car and head to work, you begin a full day of taking chances. The moment you head onto the freeway, you put enormous trust into every other person out there. When you go to your favorite restaurant, you're putting trust in the thousands of people who grew, delivered, and prepared your meal. What if a traffic light doesn't work? What if the elevator you ride in malfunctions? What if the pharmacist gives you the wrong prescription? Do you want me to go on?

Okay! What about jet airplanes? There we are hurdling five hundred miles per hour thirty thousand feet up in the air in a tin can. Now, that's taking a risk! Why are we willing to do it? Partly because everyone else does; our culture accepts it as normal. But the main reason is that in our subconscious, flying on a jet is an acceptable risk. We take risks in all aspects of our lives.

- It's taking a risk to recommit to a difficult relationship.
- It's taking a risk to tell someone you love them.

- It's taking a risk to raise children.
- It's taking a risk to commit to a new diet or exercise regimen.
- And it's taking a risk to lay it on the line and start over with a new career.

Taking risks is simply part of life. I've discovered that all of us draw different lines according to how far we're willing to jump. I know a number of people who have gone skydiving just for the thrill of it, yet they wouldn't risk it all on a new career the way I have. Conversely, I have no intention of skydiving. To me it seems like an unnecessary risk. So it's not really about what we *can* do, but rather what we *will* do.

We all have the ability to do extraordinary things, but many of us have been criticized and rejected so much that we've started to believe what we've been told. Sure, *Jump and the Net Will Appear* is about taking risks, but more important, it is a metaphor for life: Only when we take risks — those leaps of faith — can we experience the abundance life has to offer, spiritually, mentally, emotionally, even physically. The first step in creating positive change is walking away from old patterns.

But I'll tell you what this book is not about. It's not about gambling on harebrained, get-rich-quick schemes, or jumping blindly into relationships, or conjuring up half-cocked business deals. Instead it's about taking charge of our lives. I'm going to convince you that taking risks begins with taking responsibility, planning, persisting, and consistently taking action.

It's obvious that people shy away from taking risks because every time you take a risk you open yourself up to the possibility of failure. The greater the risk, the greater the failure might be. But when we take responsible risks, we enter into the flow of success, the flow of abundance. For many of us, this approach takes us way out of our comfort zone, out where failure is a very real possibility — which is also where all life's rewards are.

Change your thoughts and you change your world.

— Dr. Norman Vincent Peale

THE QUEST FOR SUCCESS

The day I left high school I set out in pursuit of a life in the music industry, lured by the temptation of fame and fortune. I was low on talent, but high on enthusiasm. I was clueless, but determined. I was caught up in the chase and the quest for success, but I did not understand the importance of self-improvement in balancing my life.

> **Living a balanced and successful life means paying equal attention to your physical, emotional, mental, and spiritual well-being.**
>
> **By making a commitment to move forward, you reclaim your power, dignity, and respect.**

I have since learned that it doesn't matter how much wind you have in your sails; if your life is incomplete and unbalanced, sailing fast will probably mean sailing off course. For many years my life was like a ship without a rudder to guide me. Just working hard and expending energy didn't bring me satisfaction and success. Over time I began to understand that it was far more important to achieve personal success than professional success. I learned that I can change my thoughts, which can change my behavior, which can change my life — and thereby enrich the lives of others. But it didn't happen overnight.

Arrogance is believing you're so high up that you
don't have to keep an ear to the ground.

— Harvey Mackay

LEARNING TO LEARN

If you had told me when I was in high school that at forty-five I would have become a perpetual student, someone who loves to learn, I would have said you were crazy. As a teenager I hated school and got poor grades. Learning was a four-letter word to me. I didn't see the point of memorizing facts and figures that were of no interest. After all, I wanted to be a recording artist. What did knowledge and learning have to do with that?

Of course, that kind of thinking was my first and biggest mistake. Learning more about the industry and learning how others before me had worked their way through the ranks could have saved me years of hardship and struggle. And being curious about everything helps you, no matter what you do. I have gone from being someone who hated the idea of learning something new to being someone who loves to learn. I have become a perpetual student. My favorite pastime is spending an hour in the self-help or business aisle at the bookstore. I'm always on a treasure hunt for new ways to improve my quality of life.

Most [people] believe that it would benefit them
if they could get a little from those who have more.

*How much more would they benefit if they could
learn from those who know more.*

— **William J. H. Boetcker**

Now, as the owner of Dark Horse Recording, I'm constantly making new friends in the music industry. We often sit around trading war stories about our adventures on the road or our dealings with record companies. I have gotten a tremendous education listening to their experiences. Over the last several years, I have had the privilege of getting to know some veteran record producers and record industry executives at the studio. During coffee and lunch breaks, I'll ask their advice and attempt to learn from their experience. In some cases, I have made major decisions based on these conversations.

I also talk to a lot of young people as they're starting their careers. Quite often I ask them about their career plans. They tell me how it's all going to turn out for them, speaking with so much confidence that they convince themselves and those around them that they *will* achieve greatness. And they *are* pretty convincing. But as I listen to them, I'm thinking, "They're making some big mistakes here. I remember when I used to think that way." I'll politely try to explain that I've been through what they're experiencing, and I begin sharing a few ideas. Unfortunately, often they're not interested in what I, or anyone else, has to say. What a shame. Imagine what we could accomplish if everyone was constantly seeking knowledge and we were all sharing what we know.

Always seek knowledge.
The secrets of success don't just present themselves
to you. You have to go out and find them.

A perpetual student is always improving,
always moving forward.

Learning from the experiences of others
helps you avoid making mistakes yourself!

CHAPTER TWO

GOING SOLO

*Only one thing is more important than learning from
experience, and that is not learning from experience.*

— Sir John M. Templeton

t was November 22, 1963, and I was in my hometown of Fort
Worth, Texas. Quite a few of my fourth-grade classmates had
gone to see our president, John F. Kennedy, speak that morning. In fact my dad, who was a salesman for Amalie Oil, left his
downtown office that morning to join the crowd gathered across
the street in an open parking lot outside the old Texas Hotel,
delighted to have a personal encounter with J.F.K. How could any-
body have known that in just a few hours he would be assassi-
nated thirty miles away in Dallas? I'll never forget watching my

teacher weeping, right in front of the class. Just like that, history was altered forever. Just like that, he was gone.

Looking back on the moments that have changed our lives helps us see the future more clearly. We say, "If only I had known then what I know now," shaking our heads, laughing and crying at the same time. People say hindsight is twenty-twenty, but I don't believe that's true. If it were, we'd quickly learn from our mistakes instead of sometimes repeating them over and over. We would use that hindsight as a priceless tool. We'd start taking better care of ourselves, we'd be more generous, we'd be more tolerant and forgiving, we'd figure out how to achieve financial independence. We'd learn to take charge of our futures.

Life was simple and predictable growing up in Fort Worth in the sixties. There was a sense of prosperity and hope. We were sending men into outer space, and Martin Luther King Jr. was leading a nonviolent civil rights movement. A fresh breeze was blowing across America. Anything seemed possible. The Ford Mustang first appeared in 1964, and my father — who has always been somewhat of a car buff — bought one. He now tells me that when he was on business trips he would wind that car up to 110 miles an hour on those flat west Texas highways.

Did you know that creating the Mustang was the event that launched Lee Iacocca's career into the stratosphere? Back then he was a young Ford executive who believed the time was ripe for a car that would appeal to the younger generation. The rest is history. Iacocca had tapped the spirit of an optimistic generation, and in doing so he ultimately became the president of Ford Motors. He later turned Chrysler around. This is a man who is not afraid to take risks.

GOING SOLO

We were young and cocky.
We saw ourselves as artists, about to produce
the finest masterpieces the world had ever seen.

— Lee Iacocca

But as far as I was concerned all the other events of that decade paled in comparison to what happened next. The Beatles landed on American soil, and pop culture was changed forever. No one, I mean no one, could have predicted this Beatlemania. It was amazing! I'll never forget watching the Beatles' debut on the *Ed Sullivan Show* one Sunday evening at my grandparents' home. There they were, John, George, Paul, and Ringo, performing "I Want to Hold Your Hand" on our little black-and-white TV set. Wow! "Listen to that music...look at those screaming girls...check out that hair!" I was hooked. I knew then and there that was the life for me — the lights, the music, the screaming fans. What an exciting life I could have if I could sing and play guitar. It all seemed so clear — this was my destiny! Of course, that night about five million other kids were thinking the same thing.

VISUALIZING, PERSISTING, AND ROCK AND ROLL

I began plotting my rise to superstardom. The first thing I did was get out my Erector Set and build a microphone stand. I managed to get a $5 Radio Shack microphone, and I taped it to the top. The thing would barely stand up, but it didn't matter. It was my first piece of gear. Now I was in show business! At eleven years old, I had chosen my path. I was a man on a mission (okay, a boy on a mission) with a vision in my head so strong that it guided the next twenty-five years of my life. Although I didn't know it, I was visualizing my future every day.

Early on it became clear that I wasn't going to make a very good front man and singer. So I started thinking that maybe I should learn to play an instrument. From time to time my folks would go out for the evening and hire a baby-sitter for my sister and me. And guess what? She brought a guitar with her! One day I purchased a Mel Bay chord book, and the next time she showed up I took up her guitar and learned every chord.

My love affair with the guitar had begun. Soon I had talked my parents into buying me my own. For hours I would strum chords, trying to see how fast I could move my hands from one position to the next. Before long I was playing dozens of Beatles songs and even starting to write a few of my own. Then I decided it was time to learn how to play standing up, but I didn't have a guitar strap. Undaunted, I took a few nails, bashed them into my poor red acoustic guitar, got a belt, hooked it on, and was on my way. I began to play in talent shows and spent hours with my friends learning songs by the Dave Clark Five, Herman's Hermits, and, of course, more by the Beatles.

Then I graduated — from elementary school — and moved on to junior high. That's when I joined a band called the Agitators, to this day one of my favorite band names. We were all seventh graders. We played at school dances and private parties for $20. That wasn't bad for those days — about five bucks apiece. Of course, back then our touring costs were extremely low. I would throw my guitar and amplifier into the trunk of my mother's car, and we were off to the big gig — perhaps someone's birthday party or the back of a flatbed truck at a Shriners' parade. We had no manager, no agent, no accountants, no lawyers, and no record company telling us they still didn't hear a radio hit.

Come to think of it, it was great! Of course, a really good rock-and-roll band never seems to last very long. Soon each member becomes convinced he is the star of the show and takes off to do his own solo project. By the eighth grade, the Agitators had reached their artistic climax, which put each of us into a fragile and delicate state. At a time when we could have become a global phenomenon, it was evident we needed to explore our artistic range and concentrate on other aspects of school life such as *finding girlfriends!*

I have always wondered which moments cause a person to make choices that alter the course of his or her life. By the end of that school year I was in a new band called Storm, and we were writing our own music together. We rehearsed constantly and took ourselves seriously. We were already learning lessons about persistence and perseverance. It became apparent to us that the way to succeed was to bear down and work hard. We were so young, but we had a sense of purpose, determination, and optimism. Those are such important attributes. To this day each of us is still playing music professionally, and I've often wondered what would have happened if we'd stayed together all these years.

A man's mind may be likened to a garden,
which may be intelligently cultivated or allowed to run wild.

— James Allen

Soon my tastes in music had evolved to include artists like Jimi Hendrix, Eric Clapton, the Animals, and a new British group called Yes. I was more obsessed, more driven, and more determined than ever to succeed. There was no doubt in my mind about my pursuit to be a big-time rock guitarist. Now I spent most of my time writing my own songs instead of learning other people's. My other friends who were serious musicians headed on to college to learn music theory and composition and to study jazz. As for me, I was hell-bent on getting as far away from school as possible. Before I had even graduated from high school, I managed to land a full-time position in a group called Great Expectations. (I know, it sounds like a dating service.) We played the nightclub circuit throughout Texas and Louisiana. We played top-forty songs and wore ridiculous jumpsuits. Yes, the seventies were upon us. Back then my goal was to be a traveling musician; so as far as I was concerned I had hit the big time: $150 a week! But just when I thought I was going straight to the top — no one can stop me now! — I got fired. I learned one thing early on: Getting into a band in which everyone would agree, get along, and put in 100 percent was never going to happen. I was still a teenager, and already I'd been in four or five bands. The moment of truth had come: It was time to go solo!

PLAYING ANYWHERE AND EVERYWHERE

Developing as a solo performer was a long, uphill climb. If you happened to visit Fort Worth about twenty-five years ago and stumbled into a disgusting hole-in-the-wall dive smelling of old beer, there was a good chance I was playing there. I played anywhere and everywhere people would listen. Branching out, I headed thirty miles east to Dallas, where I set up home in a small one-room apartment overlooking a freeway. My apartment, food, and gas expenses came to almost $250 a month, a terrifying amount at the time.

As the weeks and months went by, I called every talent agent in the phone book looking for work. Getting desperate, I'd tell them, "I'll take anything!" As fate would have it, one of them called me back with an audition. But there was a catch. It was to be at this huge Japanese restaurant called the Royal Tokyo, and it was *still under construction!* This fact most likely provided everybody in his office with a good laugh — and then an even bigger laugh when I told them I'd take it. Audition day arrived. As usual I showed up in my 1964 van, and I began unloading my guitars and sound equipment into the middle of the construction site, where I proceeded to perform for about twenty minutes. The three Japanese investors had the entire crew stop working to come listen. To make things even more interesting, the site was right beside a major freeway (not to be confused with the one that almost ran through my apartment). The roof and walls weren't even completed. What a ridiculous sight: Dallas freeway traffic a few hundred feet away, a couple dozen men in hard hats staring me down, and me playing American pop songs for a handful of Japanese men who could barely speak English!

Needless to say, it was a humbling experience. But I kept my chin up and a smile on my face until it was over. Then I returned to my apartment and tried to forget the whole thing. But guess what? Seven months later that agent called me up and almost in a tone of disbelief announced that I had the job! For the following six months I played at the Royal Tokyo, five hours each night. Each week I would hand deliver my 20 percent agency commission in person to let them know that I was going to be a force to be reckoned with.

Well, so much for that idea — they never called me with anything else. I think the Royal Tokyo would have kept me there forever if I had wanted to stay. But after six months I felt it was time for me to leave. That gig had been like a paid rehearsal, and my musical abilities had really improved. Oh, yes, and I had developed quite a taste for Japanese cuisine!

> **Risking humiliation and embarrassment usually pays off.
> If you're afraid of doing something,
> then it's probably exactly what
> you should be doing.**
>
> **Being willing to do what others won't
> will give you the competitive edge.**

DREAMING AND SCHEMING

By that time I was itching to move on, to travel, to see the world — to be heard. Someone told me I could get away with playing original material at ski resorts. So with the little money I had saved, I hit the road with a van full of gear and headed up to Colorado. I didn't have a clue about how I was going land my first engagement, so I took a job working at a guest ranch way off the beaten path, aptly called Lost Valley Ranch. It was right in the heart of the Rockies. The work — putting up fences, cutting firewood — was sometimes backbreaking. We even built a 50-foot bridge out of enormous logs that where so heavy we had to use tractors and cranes to move them.

Sometimes pain spurs us to do whatever it takes to change our circumstances for the better. If you're thinking about making changes, remember: Not taking action is what causes the *real* pain. When we procrastinate, we subconsciously believe that putting things off will be less painful than moving forward and doing what needs to be done. Once we begin to visualize the pleasure of achieving our dreams, the picture in our head will inspire us to make the change.

At least that's how it was for me. The pain of heavy physical labor was my inspiration to keep taking action until I found my next performing gig. On my days off I would drive 150 miles into Denver and knock on the doors of every booking agent I could find. I would play for them right there in their offices, and a few of those agents set up auditions for me. Once again, I would go to great lengths — sometimes driving hundreds of miles — just to set up in some club and perform a few songs for the manager. Before long my efforts paid off. Within a month I landed my first steady gig and was able to quit my job on the ranch.

Then I took off for Crested Butte, Colorado, for my first ski-resort booking. I remember crossing the treacherous Monarch Pass, where I pulled off the road and went to sleep in my van to wait out a snowstorm. When I awoke, my body was shaking so hard from the cold I could barely function. And my van was encased in three feet of snow! Not only was I unprepared, but I had no idea of the potential danger I had put myself in.

Playing ski resorts was a great experience. For a nineteen-year-old kid, getting paid to hang out with the rich and beautiful was a dream come true. That tip I got about playing in resorts turned out to be right on the money. These audiences enjoyed listening to my compositions. This inspired me to continue writing and rehearsing each day while everyone else headed for the ski slopes. But soon winter turned into spring, ski season came to a close, and I was out of work again. I've had a love affair with Colorado ever since, returning many times to play at the mountain resorts and then at some of the colleges and universities. Eventually, I had the privilege of performing at Red Rocks

Amphitheater in front of almost ten thousand people. Now that's a Rocky Mountain high!

**Sometimes pain can be our best friend
if we're willing to learn from it.**

Enthusiasm will take you farther in life than raw talent.

LEARNING THE ROPES

During the following year I performed in all kinds of situations. I was even asked to play guitar in a rock musical version of Shakespeare's *A Midsummer Night's Dream* in Chicago. During our three-month run I was introduced to what professionalism was all about. The show was a well-produced musical production with a large cast of actors, dancers, stage technicians, and, of course, other musicians. There were producers, writers, and investors all hoping the play would be such a big hit that we would soon be heading to Broadway. There was a lot of money involved, and everyone had high expectations. Tensions ran high. If I made even one mistake, a dozen people would be glaring at me in disapproval. It was a great lesson in raising my standards. I walked away from that show more focused, more professional, and a far better musician. From that experience I developed a passion for combining theatrical lighting and stage sets with my music — a key factor in later getting signed to RCA.

During my stint in Chicago I began setting my sights on moving to Los Angeles. Back then it was a revelation to discover that every major record company, management firm, and booking agency were there. Once I realized that the action was in L.A., I wanted to be a part of it. It always amazes me how easy it is to make important decisions based on feelings instead of on logic or fact. At this point I had saved up a good bit of money, which was burning a hole in my pocket. Instead of taking time to do some research or fly to Los Angeles for a few days to check it out, I simply put an idea into motion that gave me the feeling I was moving ahead.

> **Separating logic from emotion is paramount
> to making wise decisions.**
>
> **Our success in life will be in direct proportion
> to the quality of decisions we make.**

One of the most important things I want to get across in this book is how important it is to balance taking risks with careful planning. Back then I let my ignorance get in the way. Time after time I made bad decisions as I fearlessly plowed ahead. Here's another one: I decided it was time to put a band together again. No matter how impractical and unnecessary it was, I couldn't help myself. So while still in Chicago I put together a three-piece group with the idea of playing clubs for a while, working out the kinks, and then making our inevitable move West. Before I knew it, a month had turned into a year as we paid our dues on the Holiday Inn circuit, the kiss of death for any aspiring musician. If you're not careful, playing the lounges can cause musical rigor mortis to set in. To combat stagnation, we kept a strict schedule, writing and rehearsing every day.

At some hotels we were only allowed to practice after-hours, which meant that only when we finished the last set of the night, at around 2 A.M., could we begin rehearsing, which we often did until the sun came up. Then finally we'd head off to our rooms to crash. Needless to say, this was not our idea of fun. So as soon as we saved enough money, we finally headed for the Hollywood Hills — swimming pools, movie stars. Los Angeles was amazing. The sheer size of it was totally overwhelming, even terrifying. I didn't have a clue about what I needed to do to land a record deal. In the back of my mind I felt myself looking for an excuse — something to get me off the hook of facing the intimidating record industry.

**Once we raise our standards,
we look at life from a higher perspective.**

**We're drawn closer to whatever we focus on —
be it an inspiring goal or all our shortcomings.**

SIX HUNDRED SCHOOLS
IN SIX HUNDRED DAYS

That excuse came in the form of the National School Assemblies agency, which I found in the phone book under "Theatrical Agencies" my first day in Hollywood. I had heard of this agency before, and I was hopeful that this could be a way to play concerts instead of clubs. One call later we had an audition, one week later we signed a contract to tour high schools, and one month later we were back out on the road. We were hitting as many as three high schools a day, each in a different town. It was total overload: a test of endurance and stamina. Although our schedule had been planned with precision, each day was a race to see if we could pull it off at the breakneck speed required.

Playing for schools was actually a great opportunity to cut my teeth as a performer in front of large crowds. Many times we were playing in front of two to three thousand students. Wow — all of a sudden I was performing in front of fifteen to twenty thousand people a week! We lived like true gypsies, traveling in an old U-Haul truck. I built a camper in the front half, and we packed all our equipment in the rear. The front part of the truck had narrow 2-foot-wide bunk beds and a wraparound couch. It also featured an ice box that — you guessed it — ran on a block of ice. That camper was where the three of us slept, ate, and lived — our home on wheels. It looked and ran like it was on its last legs because it was! If we could get through an entire week without a breakdown, we were doing well. It would have been perfect for attending Grateful Dead concerts.

We were the personification of the *band on the run*. Every day we would wake up at five in the morning, having already parked the night before alongside the school where we were scheduled to perform. The early-morning custodian would unlock the auditorium or gym for us so we could begin setting up our gear. Once all the heavy lifting was done and we had everything in place, we would head down to the locker room for our daily shower. Many times the football team was having an early-morning practice, so there we'd be, three guys trying to be rock stars showering with the Snake River Bears or the Flagstaff Warriors. We made a contest of giving every shower at each school a rating. Some had only cold water; others were scalding. Some had almost no water pressure, while others only operated at Mach 5, shooting water with so much force that you couldn't stand in front it. Some would shoot out one tiny stream of water. Every time someone talks about how glamorous traveling must be, I think of those showers.

Then around 8 A.M. the bell would ring, a few thousand students would come rushing in, and we would kick off the day with our own brand of rock and roll. They loved us! But that's not necessarily saying much. We were playing for the entertainment deprived. The National School Assemblies had about sixty acts roaming the country playing small towns. Performers ranged from traveling snake shows, to immigrant folk dancers from Austria, to some wannabe poet reciting Longfellow. There was even a husband-wife archery show. Believe it or not, the guy would shoot a ping-pong ball off the top of his wife's head from across the room with a bow and arrow. Now *that's* a relationship that was put to the test every day! As a married man I can safely say, one way or the other, that marriage wasn't gonna last. We felt like big fishes in a bunch of small ponds. Everywhere we went we were rock stars for a day. Once, while we were setting up, a girl came up and asked Ken Wilemon — my lifelong friend and drummer — who we were. "The Beatles," he said. "Really?" she replied and then walked away with a satisfied smile.

With the help of a dozen students we would swiftly load up the truck, and in an hour's time drive fifty miles to town number two, where we would pull up to the auditorium door. There would be another dozen students ready to sling the gear onto the stage. In twenty minutes the bell would ring, students would rush in, and we would begin another concert. An hour later we would hit the final chord and, at almost lightning speed, load up again. I would get directions to the next school, and by three o'clock in the afternoon, we had performed yet a third concert. Then we would head to the town scheduled for the following morning and find a grocery store where we would purchase food and our daily block of ice. By then it would be early evening, so we would track down the school and ask if it was possible to get in the night before so we could set up and rehearse. We had a portable two-burner stove and sometimes, in below-freezing weather, we would huddle together in our little camper around our tiny table, where we would cook and warm ourselves at the same time. We would heat up a couple of pots of water, go outside, and wash our dishes. Around midnight we would bed down for five or six hours, get up the next morning, and do it all over again.

It was rock-and-roll boot camp. It made us strong. We learned how to accomplish things we thought couldn't be done. We developed a method, for instance, for setting up a couple thousand pounds of musical equipment in just minutes instead of hours. We learned that we could pull off fifteen concerts a week, a feat that in the beginning seemed impossible. Incredibly, in a year and a half we had performed at almost six hundred schools. *We had boundless energy!*

Although playing all those concerts was a great experience — especially for building our character — putting that band together was a huge distraction from learning the ins and outs of the music business. I realized later that those three years were my version of procrastination, of putting off facing what I had really set out to do. But now, at twenty-two years old, I was finally ready to head for Hollywood, this time to stay.

CHAPTER THREE

MY **BIG HOLLYWOOD**

ADVENTURE

People live by two basic philosophies: the philosophy of abundance, where anything is possible, and the philosophy of scarcity, where we look at everything through fearful eyes. For three years I procrastinated moving to Los Angeles because I was afraid. On top of that, my relatives tried to convince me that I wouldn't even land a job pumping gas. Here's what kept going through my head:

"There are already so many aspiring artists there. I'll never be noticed."

"I'm only nineteen. What do I have to offer in a place like that?"

"How will I find a place to live?"

"Will I be safe?"

"How will I make money?"

"Can I measure up to other musicians?"

"How will I get my music in the hands of the right people?"

Fear comes from anticipating the future and feeling unprepared. Your fears will begin melting away once you begin preparing. And things will get even better once you begin taking action. Because of my fears I put off moving to Hollywood for three years, but the day I finally stopped procrastinating and just did it was the day my fear finally began to disappear. And guess what? Upon arriving I discovered that most people there were quite friendly. As I started trying to make connections, I discovered that people in L.A. were starving to keep company with honest, hardworking folks with a good attitude. Of course, like any big city, L.A. was also home to people leading dark and strange lives who should be avoided. But mostly I met many wonderful people who helped and encouraged me. I realized there might even be hope for a guy like me. Imagine that!

There's a spiritual lesson to be learned here: People are basically good no matter where they live. Living in a big city doesn't automatically give people a cold heart and no conscience. In fact, some of the nicest people I've had the privilege to know, people who've become lifelong friends, I met in New York City, Chicago, and Los Angeles. In every corner of the globe, in every culture, people appreciate honesty and integrity.

For most of us L.A. conjures up images of excitement, adventure, and promise. Moving there seemed almost like a biblical quest, with California as the Promised Land. In fact, heading West in pursuit of a more prosperous life — well, that's as American as apple pie! In the 1840s, it was gold fever that brought people to California. In the 1980s and 1990s, Silicon Valley became the land of opportunity for software designers who made millions. I was simply one in a long line of Americans who moved West to make it big!

SURVIVING ᴏN DETERMINATION

Making my way through Los Angeles as a solo guitarist was like trying to sail the great oceans without knowing how to navigate. I didn't have a map, and I wasn't sure of my destination, but I was determined to get there. My persistence, sheer willpower, and enthusiasm did help me make my way through treacherous waters and ride out a few storms. As clueless as I was, my work ethic helped get me through, and I eventually made it into some of the right ports. My main problem was that at twenty-two I was convinced I knew everything. Boy, did I have a lot to learn!

Walking down Sunset Boulevard in Hollywood was a surreal experience. Any time of the day or night, you could find street performers, beggars, hookers, and religious fanatics handing out pamphlets. It was the most unusual assortment of people I'd ever seen — a melting pot of renegades, rejects, and the elite from all corners of the globe, offering up every distraction and temptation imaginable. The streets were filled with limousines and exotic cars. The billboards spotlighted the release of new rock albums or the latest action movies. Every secretary was an aspiring actress about to be discovered; every waiter had a screenplay in progress. And everyone else — well, they were all trying to break into the music business.

As soon as I hit town, I spotted a rental ad in the paper. A few hours later I was signing a lease for a one-bedroom apartment in a grand old Spanish-style building called Malaga Castle, about two blocks from Hollywood and Vine. Paramount Pictures built it in the 1930s to house the young actresses they were signing up. In one section of the four-story structure was a massive suite that had been built for Gloria Swanson. It was right out of the movies, a true slice of Hollywood. Of the tenants in the building's thirty-five units, at least twenty-five were trying to break into either the movie or the music business.

Although I was broke and living hand-to-mouth, I loved being surrounded by others who were immersed in their art. Every wannabe musician, scriptwriter, producer, director, and actor from the other forty-nine states was there with dreams of grandeur. Come on...haven't you ever imagined yourself up on the silver screen? Hasn't the dream of becoming a movie star crossed your mind at some point? Knowing that it all happened right there added to the excitement. All of us lived and breathed our art. Everyone I met was as obsessed as I was, and there was really only one subject anyone ever talked about: *show business!*

**The power of holding onto a dream
should never be taken for granted.**

**If a person has enough faith, enough desire,
enough determination and persistence,
he or she can accomplish almost anything.**

SCHOOL DAYS

Surviving in Hollywood meant learning to handle rejection every day. It's hard not to take every rejection personally when you're out there selling yourself on your talent or appearance. Learning to accept rejection was probably the most important lesson I learned in Hollywood. Here's what I discovered: *It's not what happens to us but rather how we respond to what happens that determines our success in life.*

We all know people who spend their lives denying the lessons put before them. Others embrace each lesson and turn them into stepping-stones, building a path that leads to their dreams. Life offers us a continuous stream of lessons from which to learn. Regardless of race, background, wealth, or smarts, everyone, from the cradle to the grave, experiences challenges and adversities. We all live the same twenty-four hours each day. It's our choice how we spend them. For years I spent my twenty-four hours a day learning lesson after lesson in the hardest possible way. Just when I thought I had learned them all, some new devastating challenge would arise, and instead of being at the front of the line, ready to graduate from the school of hard knocks I'd be at the back of the line again.

For seven years I worked toward my hard-knocks diploma, haunting the streets of Hollywood in pursuit of the almighty recording contract. At first, learning that there were thousands of others like me arriving daily to break into the music business really knocked the wind out of my sails. But I soon realized that everyone was the same as me: clueless. When you come to L.A. it doesn't matter what you've done in the past. Everybody starts over. Accepting this fact was especially hard for me, because I was now a cocky twenty-two-year-old, proud that I had been making a living as a guitar player since I was eighteen. My pride made me ignorant and arrogant at the same time.

During those early years in L.A., I gave it my all every day, but it wasn't nearly enough. I didn't understand how to seek out people who might have good advice to offer, people who could mentor me. I wasn't seeking knowledge, and I didn't know how to ask the right questions. If someone did offer up some good advice, I had too much pride to really listen.

Here's what I *did* have: a burning desire to succeed, big dreams, a willingness to work hard, a willingness to make sacrifices, a boatload of determination, and persistence. Here are a few mistakes that grew out of my "I know what I'm doing" attitude and that held me back:

Insecurity: "I'm not about to get a day job; I'm beyond that now."

Pride: "I'm a professional musician, and I know what I'm doing."

Denial: "As long as I stay busy, I must be making good progress."

Fear: "I can't just walk up to a record executive, introduce myself, and hand them a tape. What if they don't like it? What if they don't like me!"

I will tell you that there have been no failures in my life.
I don't want to sound like some metaphysical queen,
but there have been no failures.
There have been some tremendous lessons.

— **Oprah Winfrey**

These misconceptions led me to keep tripping over my own feet. Unfortunately, I wasted about five of my seven years in Hollywood trying to accomplish the wrong goals. If you combine that with the three years I put off moving there in the first place, well, that makes eight. Eight years of prime time! They weren't down the drain, but they weren't well spent either.

I believe all our failures happen for a reason. If we're willing to learn from them, they *do* become the building blocks of our character. Having said that, I'd also like to add that we should also be as efficient with every passing day as we can. When we have productive days, the reward is almost instantaneous. We go to bed feeling good about ourselves. Remember, the faster we learn, the faster we grow. The faster we grow, the more likely we'll succeed in achieving our dreams. That's how we begin building the momentum that moves us on the upward spiral of success in life.

It's not what happens to us, but instead how we react to what happens that makes the difference between success and failure.

Consistency builds momentum, and that momentum determines how high and how far we will go.

HANGING OUT WITH THE HELLS ANGELS

While in Hollywood my goal was to write songs, record them, and somehow along the way get discovered. Meanwhile I had to earn money. Ever since I was sixteen I had invested every dime from every gig in music equipment. At twenty-two, not only did I have an impressive collection of guitars, but I had accumulated an extensive array of sound and lighting equipment, along with that beat-up old truck to cart it around. All that gear was my biggest material asset. In fact, it was my *only* asset.

As soon I hit town I advertised "Sound and Lights for Rent" in an L.A. paper called the *Recycler*. Almost immediately the phone started ringing, and within a week I was in business.

Off I'd go in my 1964 retired U-Haul truck. Two or three days a week, I'd find myself hanging out backstage at some concert — usually heavy metal or punk — baby-sitting my equipment and people watching. For several years this is how I paid the rent, which allowed me to work on my music the rest of the time. My new rental business also gave me an up-close look at the Los Angeles music scene.

My education accelerated when I began renting my gear to a promoter of all-day rock festivals in Thousand Oaks, just outside the city. Once a month two to three thousand people would show up to see groups like Canned Heat and Steppenwolf headline after an afternoon of local band wars. One Sunday about fifty Hells Angels — that's right, the real Hells Angels motorcycle gang — showed up. It turns out they had a score to settle with some performer. When they walked right onto the stage during a performance, a hush fell over the crowd.

At first there was a little pushing and yelling, but soon it erupted into a full-scale brawl. That's when the security guards stepped in and all hell broke loose (no pun intended). It was terrifying. One guy had his head rammed into a nearby tree, as another gentleman picked up a microphone stand (yes, it was mine) and hit a stagehand so hard that the mike stand was bent around him cartoon style. Then another fight broke out over by the concession stand. People were crashing through tables as if they were in a barroom brawl in a John Wayne Western.

There I was with all my equipment right in the middle of this barbaric display of testosterone. I knew that any minute, if things got any more out of hand, my equipment could be destroyed. Luckily it only took about ten minutes for the first regiment of California state troopers to show up. They wasted no time, broke out their shotguns, and lined up the Angels against a wall, shoving the guns against their temples. Driving home that night, I thought to myself, "So this is how the West was won."

SLEEPLESS IN LOS ANGELES

My tussle with the Angels spurred me to get back to work on my music. Every possible moment I continued writing songs. Eventually I got pretty good at it. To get studio time, I traded amplifiers and guitars, or I offered to do construction work — whatever it took. This is how I began my education as a recording artist. I cranked out demo tape after demo tape, pouring my heart and soul out into every melody and lyric. I would rove around town, handing them out to the few people I assumed might be in a position to help. But if their criticism was too strong, I would retreat to my apartment like a wounded dog, and it was back to the drawing board.

Once again, I would start writing and recording a new set of songs. Day after day I kept putting one foot in front of the other. As many writers will tell you, this kind of consistency is one of the most important ways to achieve anything. You can't gain momentum without consistency. And without momentum, you can't get ahead. Have you ever heard that for every no you get, you are one step closer to a yes? As I kept knocking on doors, I proved this statement to be true. With enough knocking, I ran into a few people who thought I had promise. One young production company took more than a passing interest in my songs, and after a year of helping me improve my writing skills, they agreed to fund and produce my first real album.

Recording an album under the thumb of a producer was

harder than I ever imagined it could be. More than once I was reduced to tears as I was forced to face my shortcomings as a song-writer and recording artist. Because I had to record around their schedule, it took more than a year to finish. We settled on the title *Legend of a Fool*. Looking back, I realize that title couldn't have been more perfect. Over the next two years we did manage to sell about 7,500 copies (you'd have to be a serious collector to have one of them). Nevertheless, it was a great experience. I've always believed you can't create a great album until you make a few not-so-great ones. *Legend of a Fool* falls into the latter category.

AN ENTREPRENEUR IS BORN

Those who seldom make mistakes
seldom make discoveries.

— **Sir John M. Templeton**

Life was never dull as long as I kept my ad in the paper. Each week I found myself at some bizarre show as punk and new wave took over the music scene. Normally I would drive to the gig, set up my gear, and sit through the show. I always stayed right by my equip-ment to ensure that it wasn't abused or stolen. Then one day I got a call that changed my life in L.A.

It was from a band that wanted to rent my gear at Maverick's Flat, a hip funk and soul dance club. The club was located in Watts, one of the roughest parts of L.A. but Maverick's Flat turned out to have style and class. It was very clean and well kept, and everyone there was well dressed. They seemed like good people, and I decide to trust them with my gear. When I arrived a week later at 2:00 A.M. to retrieve my equipment and get paid, there were people everywhere, including a few bouncers who could have been pro football linebackers.

Out of a crowded room emerged a tall, good-looking man built like a brick wall. He introduced himself as John Daniels and invited me to talk with him a minute in his upstairs office. When a half dozen men followed us up the stairs, it became clear that he was the man in charge. He got right to the point. The first words out of his mouth were, "Your speaker system sounds pretty good. I want you to build me one."

"It would cost a lot. You have no idea," I replied.

"How much?" he asked.

"At least $15,000."

"Okay, build me one."

It was yet another scene out of movie where one guy's in charge and everyone else stands around looking tough. I didn't know whether or not I should take him seriously, so I said, "Well, I'd need $5,000 down." "Okay," he replied and promised to call me in a few days. Was this guy full of hot air? A few weeks later he called and told me to come by. When I returned to his office, John handed me $5,000 in cash. He didn't haggle with me; he didn't ask for an invoice; he didn't ask me to sign for it. He simply trusted me and expected that I would deliver on my promise.

Isn't it amazing that when someone trusts you with a big responsibility it makes you want to go the distance for him or her? I was so inspired to do a great job for John. Besides, he was not the kind of guy a person would want to cross. I immediately went to work by calling all over L.A. piecing together a very professional setup from used concert sound systems. The end result was a system with a value that exceeded their investment, and they were delighted with the results. And that was just the beginning. About a month later Mr. Daniels called me to his office again, led me to a small building behind Mavericks Flat, and asked me if I could turn it into a full-blown recording studio. I'm not sure what I was thinking, but I said yes.

Although I had absolutely no experience building a recording studio, John's faith in my abilities helped me believe I could do it. So I jumped. John Daniel's trust in me became my motivation to pull the whole thing off. So I surrounded myself with people who knew how to build studios, and slowly it all came together. It took the better part of a year to complete my mission, but when it was finished, once again, he just loved it. During that entire time he never asked me for a receipt of any kind. I was going through over $10,000 a month, yet John always respected and trusted me.

This experience was a great lesson in motivation. I have since learned that letting go and trusting people is the first step in allowing them to rise to their potential. So often people fall into the trap of selling themselves short and settling for less than they are capable of. Those self-limiting beliefs become the very things that hold them back. John Daniels believed that I could accomplish things I'd never done. Because of his belief in me I rose to new levels in my capability, partly because I didn't want to let him down. Another added benefit was that after I had been paid to oversee building the studio, he let me record there as often as I wanted at no charge.

The following year he asked me to build him an even bigger video studio and soundstage in yet another building. By this time I too was busy with my new band, playing dates around L.A., and chasing that almighty recording contract, but I will be forever grateful for the opportunities he gave me to grow. Those experiences as an entrepreneur taught me how to master a town that once terrified me. They also helped prepare me for building Dark Horse Recording almost twenty years later.

> **Never underestimate someone's potential when you give them the gift of trust and faith.**
>
> **Learning from the successes and failures of others is key to making quantum leaps toward our goals.**

Creative positive expectation!...
If the schools in this country would teach children
to look for the best and believe they could accomplish the best,
they would be the best, and we would have the greatest
country in the history of mankind.

— Dr. Norman Vincent Peale

CHAPTER FOUR

ALMOST FAMOUS

When I moved to Hollywood I observed famous and successful people from a distance. Then I went to work for them, first as a stagehand, then as a sound engineer, and later as a limousine driver. Years later, as a musician and performer, I toured with these same people as an opening act for their concerts. Now, twenty years later, as a recording artist I collaborate with them on my records, and as a recording studio owner I enjoy their visits to Dark Horse Recording. I am now working with some of the same people I used to chauffeur around Los Angeles. More than once I've had the pleasure to reminisce with them about the days when I was their driver.

It's amazing how working hard *does* pay off and how nothing's more satisfying than when things come full circle. Throughout this book I talk a lot about the importance of "working smart." I've come to the conclusion that *not* working smart holds more people back from achieving the life they want than anything else. Learning to focus and clearly plan as you work will make your hard work pay off exponentially.

As for me, after six years of living in L.A. I had still not managed to achieve my goal of landing a major recording contract. It was becoming more and more apparent that I was doing something wrong. But what? I worked hard, I believed in my musical abilities, I was living where the action was — but it obviously wasn't enough. Eventually I began to realize that just because I was kicking up a lot of dust, it didn't mean that I was getting any closer to my goals. After years of making excuses, I had to face the truth: I still didn't know what I was doing.

THE POWER OF A NEW THOUGHT

When I was young, success seemed like some mystical experience reserved for the chosen few. It seemed unachievable. Clearly I wasn't thinking the right thoughts. The reason most people don't attract success into their lives is because of their thinking. (I'll discuss this concept further in the next chapter.) Just working hard to achieve my goals wasn't enough. I was still thinking the same thoughts I had years before. There's an old saying: "You can't get where you've never been by doing the same things you've always done." The same goes with our thoughts. We have more than 30,000 thoughts a day; the problem is that 29,900 of them are the same tired ones we thought yesterday. We can't ascend to new heights without lifting our thoughts to new heights.

I didn't realize it then, but it took being totally frustrated from beating my head against the wall for me to begin changing my thinking. The irony was I'd spent the last six years in the right place, but the world I wanted to enter still seemed just out of my reach. That's when I began asking a new question: How could I surround myself with the right people? Strangely enough, the answer appeared in the form of a real job: I became a limousine driver! My strategy was to earn money while rubbing shoulders with the movers and shakers of Hollywood, to learn about their world. Guess what? That's exactly what happened. It was the perfect job for someone trying to break into the music industry. All of a sudden, I was driving some of the biggest stars in the world, hanging out at lavish Hollywood parties, and getting paid for it!

CLOSE ENCOUNTERS

But that's not how it started out. When you first start driving for a limo service, you get all the unimportant after-hours assignments. At 3:00 A.M. I'd get a call: "Can you be at the airport in an hour?" Los Angeles International Airport was almost an hour's drive from Hollywood, so I'd jump out of bed, throw on my one and only three-piece suit, and scramble to make it on time. It wasn't uncommon for me to drive for sixteen hours, go home, fall into bed, and an hour later get a call from the dispatcher asking me once again to be at the airport in an hour!

At first the schedule was brutal, but I took everything they threw at me, and in just a few months I worked my way up to a first-call driver. What a great lesson that was! If you're willing to go the extra mile, in my case literally, be dependable, and work hard, then you *will* stand out. Just the fact that I never said no and was always ready to work impressed them enough to start assigning me to their "A list." Soon I was driving some of the biggest celebrities in the world and even getting to know some of them. I drove Christopher Reeve, Mike Wallace, Pat Benatar, Mike Douglas, Melissa Manchester, Dolly Parton, Richard Pryor, Carol Burnett, and countless others — even Benji the dog! But the best part was the education I got about the inner workings of Hollywood.

Almost everyone I drove was polite and gracious. One time Pat Benatar invited me in to have tea. Christopher Reeve and I talked up a storm one afternoon as I drove him home from a television interview. Melissa Manchester invited me to a birthday party she was having. The more successful they were, the more warm and accessible they were. I began to realize that the ones who had achieved the most were also the ones who enjoyed letting down their guard and talking. I began to think that maybe it was one of the reasons they were so successful in the first place.

Was landing that job a lucky twist of fate? I don't think so. One of God's greatest gifts to us is the free will to make our own decisions. Sometimes we procrastinate making those decisions for years until the pressure gets so great that we're willing to change course. But the choice is always ours to make.

**When you're willing to go the extra mile,
be dependable, and work hard, you *will* stand out.**

**Luck is what happens when opportunity
and preparation meet.**

THE ART OF PREPARATION

When I wasn't busy driving the rich and famous, I was in constant rehearsal with a five-piece band I had assembled in hopes of getting a record contract. Like countless other bands we showcased around L.A. playing for free just to be heard. Every musician out there pretty much had the same dream: to become a member of a hit act, tour the world traveling first class, perform before thousands of people a night, and get paid lots of money for it!

Of all the musicians I worked with during my time in California, I know of only one who went on to live that rock-and-roll fantasy: Jim Ingle. Jim was my band mate and partner for the four years that we slugged it out in L.A. Almost every day we rehearsed in an empty warehouse in Watts provided by my friends at Maverick's Flat, where we constantly hammered out new songs. Jim had always been the first one to arrive at rehearsal. He had a great attitude even in the toughest of times and was professional to a fault. During the four years we worked together, he was constantly finding ways to improve not only his drumming and singing skills but also his visual performance. Over time he began to stand out, with his blend of creative, rock-solid style and striking showmanship. You couldn't take your eyes off him. Whether we were playing at a small club where no one seemed to even pay attention, or in front of thousands, Jim always gave everything he had.

From time to time we managed to lure a few music business bigwigs to hear us perform. A few of them even made us some grandiose promises, but in the end nothing ever panned out. So after four years, we finally decided that we had given it our best shot and that it was time for each of us to move on. That's when I left L.A. for good. But Jim's career was about to take off like a rocket.

It wasn't too long before Jim had an incredible opportunity to audition for the Pointer Sisters. He showed up at a Los Angeles soundstage along with a handful of other drummers who were all hoping to be chosen to hold the groove for one of the hottest acts of the decade — at a time when their album *Break Out* was at the top of the charts. Although another drummer was initially chosen, a few weeks later Jim got a call saying they wanted to hear him again. But for *this* audition there was some added pressure.

Because the group was in the middle of a national tour and because of the sudden absence of their drummer, Jim's audition was to perform with the Pointers for an entire live concert! He was sent a tape of the show but had only about forty-eight hours to prepare and get himself and his drums up to Valley Forge, Pennsylvania, where they would be performing in the round at the Valley Forge Music Fair. The rest was up to him.

Imagine having to lay it all on the line in front of thousands of people who bought tickets expecting a flawless performance. But Jim was *prepared.* For the year after our band dissolved he had been practicing endlessly to be ready whenever opportunity did come his way. He was already a killer drummer, but he still spent countless hours developing his ability to hold down a rock-steady groove — an essential ability when you're the driving force behind the rhythmic dance music of a group like the Pointer Sisters.

Jim had already outfitted his drums with flight cases just in case something ever came up. Something came up all right! Not only did he fly his drums across country, but that flight was the beginning of a journey that changed the course of his life. Because of Jim's incredible preparation, not only did he pass the audition, but he kept his gig with the Pointers for fourteen years, traveling and performing all over the world! Just one month after his audition, the Pointers were presented with two American Music Awards, sending their popularity into orbit. They were now playing nothing but the biggest and most prestigious venues. They had become one of the most successful headlining acts in the world, and Jim was a part of it.

I remember seeing all this for the first time when they came to Nashville. At one point in the show Jim was featured playing an extended drum solo. There he was, in front of more than ten thousand people, with his pounding rhythms blasting out over the huge concert speakers as dozens of spotlights focused on him. I stood there thinking, "Way to go, Jim!" Was it luck that got him that sought-after position? I don't think so. I believe it was a combination of many things working together, starting with his thorough *preparation*. Also:

- **Determination**
- **Diligence**
- **Perseverance**
- **Consistency**
- **Integrity**
- **Professionalism**
- **Talent**

Notice that I put talent at the end of the list. This is not to take away from Jim's extraordinary musical ability, but simply to point out that without these other qualities it's quite likely that Jim would still be one of thousands of other drummers in L.A. wondering why they haven't gotten their big break. "Everyone will have an opportunity cross their path sooner or later," he once told me. "The trick is to be prepared."

The price of success is much lower
than the price of failure.

Live each moment as if all eyes are on you.

CHAPTER FIVE

CHANGING ᴏᴜʀ MINDS

*The greatest revolution of our generation
is the discovery that human beings,
by changing the inner attitudes of their minds,
can change the outer aspects of their lives.*

— William James

A few months ago I was ordering lunch at a local restaurant. The waitress was so delightful that my friend and I both commented on how good she made us feel with no more than a smile and a cheerful voice. A few weeks later at that same restaurant I encountered a waiter who had the exact opposite effect. I began cracking a few jokes in the hopes that he might break a smile, but I was unsuccessful. He might have been sleep deprived or just have had a fight with his girlfriend. Maybe he was running a 103-degree fever, or he had just received some devastating news. I'll never know, so I shouldn't judge him, but to some degree I still do. It's human nature.

Within minutes of meeting someone, we often develop strong opinions about them based simply on their attitude. A person's attitude is their imprint on everyone they meet. Even in the worst of times, people who have cultivated a winning attitude will have a positive influence on those around them. Their attitude becomes the window to their soul.

We associate many traits with successful people: self-discipline, persistence, focus, consistency, optimism. But the most important trait of all is attitude. If you're interested in getting the most of your life, attitude is the place to start.

> **A great attitude will take you from apathy to enthusiasm, indifference to passion, sarcasm to optimism.**
>
> **Your attitude is the launching pad for every success and failure you'll ever have.**

Why does one person have so much passion for life that she gets up early and stays up late to pursue her dreams, while another finds it difficult to even get out of bed without complaining? It boils down to the quality of our attitudes. The only way we will change our world is to change our thoughts.

Of all the beautiful truths pertaining to the soul
which have been restored and brought to light in this age,
none is more gladdening or fruitful of divine promise

and confidence than this — that [we are]
the master of thought, the molder of
character, and the maker and shaper of condition,
environment, and destiny.

— James Allen

IT'S YOUR CHOICE

Never forget that attitude is a choice. Abraham Lincoln once said, "A person will be just about as happy as they make up their minds to be." It's amazing how everything in our lives takes a new direction once we realize we have complete control over our thoughts and attitude. It took a long time for this truth truly to sink in for me. The day I looked in the mirror and made a choice to change my attitude was the day I truly began changing my life. It's now clear that this profound distinction marks the most important crossroad for each one of us. Think about it. God gave us the ability to choose how we feel about everything that happens to us. God gave us the ability to choose which direction we wish to go in life. It's our choice if we wish to do the least we can get away with or to create an extraordinary life for ourselves.

As a business owner, I now have four people on staff and as many as twelve interns at any time. I've learned firsthand how important a great attitude is to business success. In fact, I have come to believe that attitude is more important than aptitude. During the last six years we've had more than 150 interns work here as their last step before graduating with a degree in studio engineering. Most of our staff was picked from those interns. The ones with the best attitude are the ones who rose right to the top. To me, attitude is more important than technical expertise about equipment. At the end of the day attitude is more important to me than anything else. A great attitude is infectious; it changes the way a business operates, and you can't put a price on that.

ATTITUDE MATTERS EVEN IN SHOW BUSINESS

In my early years in Hollywood I thought that a "rock-and-roll" attitude bred success. I thought you had to act like you didn't care about anyone or anything. Many famous people have in fact built careers on adolescent behavior, with no regard for anyone but themselves. But in the long run those people have almost always paid a high price for their arrogance. It's fascinating and sobering to hear stories of people who at one time were on top of the world but now are worse off than when they started — taking odd jobs and living in the past. Some of them confess openly how they failed to appreciate what had been handed to them and acknowledge how they hurt those around them. In the long run their bad attitudes gave back to them exactly what they had dished out. Remember the old saying, "You meet the same people on the way up as you do on the way down"?

A perfect example of someone who built success with a great attitude is Dolly Parton. When I was only twenty-one and first living in L.A., I worked for three months in a big rehearsal facility where rock acts such as Led Zeppelin and Fleetwood Mac rehearsed before leaving on tour. Early one morning I arrived to find a tour bus with a butterfly painted on the back parked outside the loading dock. It was Dolly's.

I was sent over to escort her to the rehearsal stage. The first thing that stood out to me was how incredibly polite she was. It was obvious she had been riding all night and was in need of sleep, a shower, and breakfast, but that didn't dampen her pleasant demeanor. She didn't have to smile, be polite, or even acknowledge my existence, but she did all those things, leaving an impression on me I never forgot. Six years later, as a limo driver, I drove her to the Beverly Hills Hotel after her appearance on *The Mike Douglas Show*. She was promoting her new movie, *Nine to Five*. By this time she had become a true international superstar. As she headed from the television studio to the limousine, an army of people followed her. She was on top of the world, but she was still gracious and courteous to everyone she came in contact with — including me.

A few years ago my son, Joseph, asked me during breakfast, "Who's in the studio today?" "Dolly Parton," I answered. Things sure have come full circle. Twenty years ago it would have been hard to imagine Dolly Parton coming to our farm to work on one of her albums. Later that day I shared with her how our paths had crossed several times before. Her face lit up with pleasure. Now every time I see her, or even hear her name mentioned, I always walk away thinking about her delightful attitude.

> *Science may have found a cure for most evils;*
> *but it has found no remedy for the worst of them all —*
> *the apathy of human beings.*

> — Helen Keller

OPTIMISM ᴠꜱ. PESSIMISM

One of the things I enjoy about living in a music city is watching all the newcomers with dreams of hitting it big as recording artists. Ninety-nine percent of them don't have a clue about how hard it really is or how incredibly slim the odds are, yet they persist, fueled by incredible optimism. If they really sat down and thought about how many tens of thousands of other hopefuls are also trying to become the next Faith Hill or the next Sting, they would likely give up and go home. Instead they stay focused on their dream. Their optimism is so strong that they keep on trying — even in the face of overwhelming odds.

The odds against success in the music industry are so huge that a few years ago I came to the conclusion that Dark Horse Recording is really a kind of country club for lottery winners. The people who make it to my studio to record high-budget records beat the same odds as lottery winners do. But you know what? In this business pessimists would never make it this far. They would not stand a chance. In the music industry, as in life, the rewards go to those who keep on swinging until they hit the ball out of the park — no matter the odds.

> *The pessimist sees difficulty in every opportunity.*
> *The optimist sees opportunity in every difficulty.*
>
> **— Winston Churchill**

So many people believe that circumstances control their lives. But it's our thoughts that shape our future. It's our thoughts that fuel our passion and courage to go out and pursue our dreams. An optimistic attitude can change everything. An optimist will always win out over a pessimist by focusing on the positive. Believing they'll succeed, optimists try over and over until that's exactly what happens. So next time, instead of blaming circumstances, lift up your thoughts, and see how they reshape your circumstances.

CHANGING ᴏᴜʀ MINDS

FROM COUSIN JED'S GUITAR SHED TO
MICHAEL JACKSON'S WORLD TOUR

If you're still not convinced that attitude can redirect your life, check out this story about Dave Graef. Dave was a college student who, through his positive attitude and his habit of always going the extra mile, became an extraordinary success in a very short amount of time.

In the fall of 1985 I was scheduled to perform at Graceland College in Lamoni, Iowa. Back then I was traveling alone in my orange Chevy van. When I would pull onto a campus, ten or so college students would volunteer to help me set things up. On this particular day I arrived late. With only an hour until show time I was somewhat frantic to get things ready. Looking around at my crew of volunteers I asked, "Is there someone who might be able to tune up my thirteen guitars?" In an almost synchronized gesture all the students pointed to a young man named David Graef. So I handed him a piece of paper and asked, "Hey, David can you tune these guitars to the different tunings I've written down here?" He just smiled and said, "No problem." For the next hour I scrambled to hook up my sound equipment and get everything in place so I could change clothes before show time.

In my haste, I'd totally forgotten about the young man I had put in charge of my guitars. But just as I finished my sound check he came up to me and announced that he was done. The audience was already filing into the auditorium, so I didn't even have time to double-check his work. As the concert began and I walked on stage, I picked up my first guitar and was relieved to discover that it was in perfect tune! As I continued to play one guitar after the other, I realized that each instrument had been polished, the necks and frets had been wiped down, and, of course, they had all been precisely tuned.

David had done three important things:

1. He had demanded a high level of excellence of himself.
2. He had gone the extra mile by giving more than was expected.
3. And he had done it all with a smile on his face, expecting nothing in return.

David's commitment to excellence, willingness to go the extra mile, and great attitude caused him to stand out from the hundreds of students I met each year who volunteered as stagehands. As we were packing up, I began telling Dave what an outstanding job he'd done, and he told me what a passion he had not only for working with guitars but also for playing them. He proceeded to invite me to his dorm room, where he proudly showed me an acoustic guitar he was building from scratch. Needless to say, he left me with a powerful impression, so over the next two years I stayed in touch with him. Although David was already outstanding at working with guitars, he had no concept that it was possible to do it professionally. He had grown up on a large farm in West Texas and didn't know there were people who made a living building and repairing guitars for rock stars. He had no idea there were people who toured with big pop acts maintaining their instruments. But he was about to find out in a big way and, as you will see, his attitude more than made up for his lack of knowledge.

In 1987 he graduated from Graceland and began working in a music store called — get this — Cousin Jed's Guitar Shed in

Independence, Missouri. That's when I offered him a job to travel with me as my guitar tech and stage manager. For six months we traveled and worked together, and he ensured that my concerts ran smoothly. David had such a positive attitude that sometimes I teased him about it. Everywhere we went he made friends. As my ambassador, he not only made me sound good, but he made me look good too. Imagine the impact that kind of attitude would have on your boss, your spouse, your child, or a stranger. There is a tremendous source of strength in understanding the power of attitude. It is a distinction that empowers us to experience all that life has to offer, to take charge of our destiny, to make a difference. Remember, our life is a reflection of our attitudes. With a positive attitude you will create positive results.

Once our tour was over, Dave wanted to establish himself in Nashville as both a guitar tech and a guitar player. So I introduced David to my friend Greg Krochman at Nashville's best guitar repair shop, the Classic Ax. After David showed Greg how serious and dedicated he was about working on guitars he was hired. His quality workmanship and winning attitude quickly built his reputation with many of the country stars who brought their guitars there.

Your living is determined not so much by what life brings to you as by the attitude you bring to life.

— John Homer Miller

By the next year Dave began taking leaves of absence to tour with the Oak Ridge Boys as their guitar tech. At that time there was nobody bigger in country music. By 1991 he began traveling full-time with Wynonna. But just as David's career was looking unstoppable, he suffered a devastating setback. One night he pulled over to help someone who was stranded on the side of the road. As he was facing downhill digging into his truck for a tire jack, a parked car about fifty feet uphill from him began silently rolling toward David, and it ran into him, crushing his legs. The damage was so extensive the doctors didn't know if he would be able to walk again. I remember visiting him just after his accident, and even in his uncertainty about whether he would walk again, he kept a smile on his face. He never said a negative word. He didn't allow himself to be controlled by his debilitating circumstances.

A few weeks later, even though he still couldn't walk, Dave helped out on a local showcase involving Gary Chapman. David had to sit the entire time with his feet propped up in enormous leg braces. All he could do was tune and restring the guitars that were brought to him. Nonetheless, everyone was so impressed with him that night that he was offered a tour with Michael W. Smith, starting almost immediately. David reminded them, "Now, you realize that I can't walk?" "We know that," they replied. "But the job's yours if you want it." Well, David took the job and as the seventy-five-city tour progressed, his legs slowly started to improve until he was finally walking again. As that tour came to an end, he was offered a job as guitar tech traveling with Amy Grant's band for the next year. I remember thinking to myself, "Boy, everyone sure loves David!"

Nothing can stop the man with the right mental attitude from achieving his goal; nothing on earth can help the man with the wrong mental attitude.

— W. W. Ziege

By the end of Amy's tour David was not only fully recovered, but he was getting offers from the biggest touring acts to take care of their guitars. By 1994, just six years after he moved to Nashville, David could pick and choose almost any artist or band in the world he wanted to tour with. So the next year he signed up to go on Michael Jackson's worldwide Dangerous Tour, participating in one of the biggest events in pop music history. An army of musicians, dancers, and crew flew from country to country in five private jumbo jets, and David was a part of it.

But David's story keeps getting better. All this time as a guitar tech, he was constantly practicing and preparing as a guitarist. Eventually opportunity knocked. You see, Michael Jackson's guitar player looked great on stage, but he couldn't always play the difficult solos and concentrate on showmanship at the same time. So David was asked to perform those parts from behind the amplifiers to complete the band's sound. He sat backstage playing some of the most difficult guitar solos, allowing others to look and sound good. For David it wasn't about the glory but about achieving excellence. Listen, when those stadiums erupted with applause, although it wasn't directed at David, Michael Jackson knew who was playing those solos.

Who would have guessed just a few years earlier that this mild-mannered college student would end up working with the biggest stars in the world and earning a salary to match. When the Dangerous Tour finally wrapped up, David received offers from the Stones, Yes, Pink Floyd, and Phil Collins, but he turned them all down. He was ready to come out from behind the amplifiers and take his place on stage. Now David is touring with some of the same major acts as he was before — no longer as a guitar tech but as a featured guitar player. In fact, I called him on his cell phone the other day and asked him where he was. "I'm backstage at Madison Square Garden," he said, "preparing for sound check!"

"Great show business story, Robin," you might be saying, "but I live in the real world. What does this have to do with me?" Listen, David achieved success not just because he could tune and repair guitars better than anyone else, but because he practiced the same principles of success that apply to anyone in any field: setting high standards, demanding excellence of himself, going the extra mile, and, most important, having an outstanding attitude. Remember, when you maintain a winning attitude, sooner or later just like Dave, you'll get the chance to shine.

**The quality of our thoughts equals
the quality of our lives.**

**It's worth saying again: It's not what happens to us
that shapes our destiny, it's how we react to those events.**

CHAPTER SIX

YES!

Prove yourself
You are the move you make
Take your chances win or lose...
Be yourself
Give your free will a chance
You've got to want to succeed...
Look before you leap
And don't hesitate at all.

— "Owner of a Lonely Heart," Rabin,
Jon Anderson, Squire, Horn

G reat opportunities come to all of us, but so often we miss them completely. Every day we have hundreds of chances to say something kind, to do something helpful, to make a difference. Every time you seize an opportunity you are making an investment in your success, in your future. Remember, your ability to work hard and to be prepared will be in direct proportion to the opportunities that will appear before you. This chapter is about how I put myself on the line — how I jumped and how my net appeared. I didn't put my life or livelihood on the line; really I just risked looking stupid. But the payoff was greater than I had ever imagined it could be. This is the story of how I crossed paths with my musical hero and how I learned the value of seizing the moment before it passed by. Sometimes an opportunity presents itself only once, and if you're willing to risk rejection and take a leap of faith, you can change the course of your life.

Yes is one of the most extraordinary pop-rock bands of all time. Since the late sixties they have endured three decades of trends, critics, and the public's fickleness. Since the day I heard them for the first time I have been their biggest fan. Those high, angelic harmonies against the backdrop of their complex instrumentation were unlike anything I had heard before. I was awestruck! When their album *Fragile* was released, which included the classic six-minute hit "Roundabout," I spent hours sitting between my stereo speakers entranced by its majesty. It was a musical awakening for me.

At the same time that other bands were pushing the boundaries of vulgarity and sexuality, Yes took the higher road. Their music took the textures of complex classical motifs and crafted them into high-energy rock. It was the most inspiring music I had ever heard. Their musical craftsmanship was of a higher caliber than most of what was being played on the radio.

I wasn't alone in my feelings. For many musicians of my generation, Yes became the standard by which we measured ourselves. Each player in Yes was a virtuoso in his own right, and when all that extraordinary talent was combined, it produced something truly unique. In fact, the term *progressive rock* was coined to describe their music. The creative force of this legendary band was lead singer and co-writer Jon Anderson, a man who possessed a clear, high voice unlike any I have heard to this day. His uplifting lyrics blended philosophical and spiritual ideas. As I was developing and maturing as a guitarist and songwriter, it was his creativity and positive approach to melody and lyrics that were my greatest influence. I fantasized that some day I would meet and play guitar with Jon Anderson.

> *It is difficult to say what is impossible,*
> *for the dream of yesterday*
> *is the hope of today*
> *and the reality of tomorrow.*
>
> — **Robert H. Goddard**

VISUALIZING THE FUTURE

The first time I ever saw Yes in concert was in front of a sold-out crowd at Anaheim Stadium just outside Los Angeles. It was the summer of 1975, and I had just moved to Los Angeles after finishing up my two-year National School Assemblies tour. When I heard that Yes was coming to southern California, I was ecstatic. It was to be an all-day event starting with the classic rock group Gentle Giant, then Gary Wright, who had a new hit on the charts called "Dream Weaver," followed by Peter Frampton, who was riding the crest of a wave with his mega-hit album *Frampton Comes Alive*, and then the main event: Yes.

The concert had festival seating, which means there were no

reserved seats. Whoever shows up first gets the best shot at sitting close to the stage. I arrived at the stadium the evening before, figuring I would be one of the first in line. Was I ever surprised to discover thousands of people who had arrived before me, also prepared to stay the night. By midnight there must have been at least ten thousand fans already spread out on the pavement, creating a seemingly endless river of people in the mammoth stadium parking lot. A thick fog had now set in, which added an eerie glow to the parking lot lights. It was a surreal experience to spend the night with all those people, but nothing compared to the crush of bodies flooding into the stadium once the gates opened the next morning. Tens of thousands of people rushed onto the open field as everyone claimed a small patch of ground, about one or two square feet, for themselves. There was no room to move. It was an unbelievable sea of humanity.

It seemed like forever waiting for the music to begin, but finally around noon Gentle Giant took to the stage and gave a jaw-dropping performance. Next Gary Wright came on, followed by Peter Frampton, who, to the crowd's delight, rattled off all his hit songs. It was a wonderful afternoon of music, but then at last the long-awaited moment arrived. The sun was just setting over the stadium when the towering stacks of speakers erupted with Stravinsky's *Firebird Suite*. The giant stage set came alive as hundreds of spotlights began firing to the rhythm of the music. Then thousands of flashing cameras from the audience began to answer back as if engaging in some extraterrestrial conversation. Four powerful laser beams appeared from behind the drums and stretched across the stadium as the audience exploded in applause. The crowd was electrified. With chills running down my spine, I remember thinking, "This is incredible, and Yes isn't even out here yet!"

As the five band members came out onto the stage, the cheer from 55,000 ecstatic Yes fans was deafening. Jon Anderson was wearing a long white robe, the perfect complement to his voice and lyrics. When they kicked in with their first song, I was absolutely mesmerized, and I wasn't alone. We were witnessing five of the most incredible musicians playing completely in sync. Yet it was clearly Jon's band. As I watched and listened, I imagined myself playing guitar alongside him. I imagined myself writing songs with him. I imagined recording an album together. On the one hand the idea seemed too far-fetched to entertain seriously, but on the other, I could see it as a possibility. What an amazing night!

That's how visualizing begins. Until you can picture your goal in your head, chances are slim that it will ever come to pass. Athletes have known this for years. That's why a football coach will take video footage of a player and edit together only the best plays... then have that player watch himself over and over at his very best. In essence he visualizes himself as an outstanding player, sending a powerful message to his subconscious about his capabilities.

> **Use your imagination to plan out your life
> like a movie script — your life as you want it to be.**
>
> **Every new reality begins with your imagination.**

OPPORTUNITY KNOCKS

Imagination is more important than knowledge.

— **Albert Einstein**

A decade later, Yes was still going strong. In fact, the group had gone through a few changes and resurfaced sounding even better than ever. Their smash hit "Owner of a Lonely Heart" had captured a new generation of fans. Yes had now joined a very small group of seventies rock acts whose popularity spread into the eighties. Jon's voice was sounding impeccable, and their new songs reflected changing trends without losing their musical essence. Depth, substance, and conviction were still what this band was all about.

By this time, my career as a recording artist had started to blossom. I now had four national albums under my belt and was living in Nashville, but I spent most of my time on the road touring college campuses. Once or twice my traveling schedule intersected with Yes's, giving me the chance to see them. In February 1988 I learned that they were coming to the downtown arena in Nashville, and I was going to be in town. Like thousands of other Yes fans, I bought my tickets, anxious for another chance to hear them. Finally the day of the concert arrived.

Does this sound like an opportunity knocking? Well, I didn't yet see it as that, but that's what it was. I couldn't stop thinking about how incredible it would be if I could somehow meet Jon Anderson. "What if I could play him some of my music? What if he liked it? What if somehow, someday, we could actually work together?" Like ten years before, it seemed too far-fetched to seriously entertain. After all, he was British and probably lived across the ocean and was constantly touring all over the world. Why would someone like that have any interest in working with someone like me? It all seemed completely impossible.

Nonetheless, I phoned up my friend and fellow Yes fan Mark Hollingsworth. I confessed to him how frustrated I felt being so close and yet so far from being able to meet Jon. Mark encouraged me to take a chance and try somehow to meet him. Let me rephrase that — he *challenged* me to take a risk and make the effort, even at the expense of looking foolish. Being a consultant in the music industry, he reminded me how he had met some other major acts by simply tracking them down backstage — high-profile performers who are now good friends. "What do you have to lose?" he asked.

Although it was not in my nature to be so aggressive, I knew he was right. Now I was staring opportunity in the face. My first reaction was to convince myself it wasn't the right time or that I wasn't quite prepared. I kicked and squirmed, but I couldn't ignore Mark's challenge. So as I left for the concert, I grabbed a cassette tape containing rough mixes from the album I was working on. I stuffed the tape, a piece of notebook paper, and a pen in my pocket and headed out the door.

Many do with opportunities as children do at the seashore,
they fill their little hands with sand,
and then let the grains fall through, one by one,
till all are gone.

— Thomas Jones

Although the concert was great, I couldn't fully enjoy it. I stood there in torment the whole time, knowing I had to talk to Jon. I had to create my own opportunity and there could be no procrastinating. The time was now! As Yes broke into "Roundabout," the song they had been using as an encore for years, that was my cue. I scribbled a few words on that piece of notebook paper, stuffed it into the cassette box, and headed down to the floor level to begin trying to talk my way backstage.

The fact that I'm a performer and somewhat experienced in getting around these events usually gives me *some* edge. But no matter whom I talked to or what I said, I could not convince anyone to let me backstage. So I went up to the sound man. After I relayed my story to him, he promised to give the tape to Jon himself. "That's it," I thought, as I handed it to him. "I can't get backstage. Now my tape is gone and will probably go straight in the trash."

By now they were playing their third encore, and I knew that my narrow window of time was almost up. So in one last-ditch effort, I exited the coliseum into the freezing February night and circled around to the back of the arena. Over in the loading area where equipment trucks and buses were standing by, a policeman was sitting just inside a glass door. I rapped on the window to get his attention, and he cracked open the door to see what I wanted, just as Yes was hitting the last chord for the night. The next instant I looked down the corridor, and to my surprise saw Jon Anderson about fifty yards away being ushered down a ramp from the stage by two security guards.

When it comes to seizing moments like this, the shy and introverted Robin would usually run the other way. This time my instincts must have taken over, and without thinking about it I yelled out, "Jon!" loud enough to be heard over the still-roaring crowd. He looked over, our eyes met, and he motioned for me to be let in, at which point one of those men walked over and said that Jon was headed for his dressing room and would see me in a bit.

FACE TO FACE

About forty-five minutes later my musical mentor emerged, walked over, smiled, and said hello. There I was, face-to-face with

Jon Anderson. For so long I had dreamed of this moment, of the deep thoughts and mysteries of life we would share. Instead I was completely tongue-tied. I couldn't even get simple words to come out of my mouth. It was humiliating. Others were standing around as well, causing me to be more inhibited than I already was. It was like a good dream gone bad.

Finally, I said, "I'm a jazz guitar player, and I'm almost finished with my newest album. I gave a rough copy to your sound man. If he gives it to you, and if you like it, would you ever consider working with me?" Well, now I had done it! I had put him on the spot, and his response was to say nothing. It was torture standing there with my foot in my mouth. Then someone else started talking to him, and I just stood there staring at him like a cow at a passing train. After a while I blurted out the same message again.

I said, "Jon, if you *really* like my music, would you consider working with me?"

He just looked at me, sighed, and said, "Well, anything is possible."

If you looked up *awkward* in the dictionary, this moment would be the definition. What did I expect him to say? He didn't know me from Adam, and although I wanted to say so much, nothing was coming out right. So I said good-bye and headed home.

The next day I left for a one-week tour of colleges in the upper Midwest. As the miles passed by one by one, I reflected on my encounter with Jon, thinking, "Boy, I really blew it, and that's probably the last time I'll see him." But as you've probably surmised by now, this wasn't the end of my story; in fact, it was just the beginning. A week later I returned home, and like always I headed directly to my answering machine. There it was — my very first message. I could hardly believe it! It was Jon's distinctive voice, British accent and all, telling me not only that he liked my music but also that he thought maybe we could work on some songs together. *Wow! I mean wooooooooow!* For me there was no bigger thrill. If Elvis Presley, John Lennon, and Jimi Hendrix had all reappeared one last time just to sing on my record, it wouldn't have compared to this moment.

As I sat there playing that message over and over, it hit me what an incredible lesson I had learned. *When you take a risk and seize an opportunity, no one can predict the outcome. But you know exactly what will happen if you don't — nothing.* As excited as I was, I knew that pursuing this relationship further wouldn't be easy. On his message Jon had left the number of their management firm in Los Angeles. From there I had to go through a maze of calls, explanations, and messages just to talk with him a second time. Cultivating a relationship with a man who is almost always traveling somewhere in the world took a lot of patience and persistence. But eventually my determination paid off.

After I spent *years* consistently writing songs for him and mailing him tapes, Jon invited me to Los Angeles, where I became a member of his band as we rehearsed together for a Jon Anderson solo tour of China. There I was, standing right alongside Jon playing "Owner of a Lonely Heart," enjoying his crystal-clear voice singing out over the speakers, and I remember thinking, "It doesn't get any better than this!"

Learn to listen.
Opportunity could be knocking at your door very softly.

— **Frank Tyger**

Several years later Yes came to Nashville on tour once again. But this time I went to the concert as Jon's guest! After the show we

talked backstage, working out details for an album we were planning to record together. Meanwhile the crew was busy loading up
the huge stage equipment into a row of tractor trailers. I couldn't
help but think back to that summer concert more than twenty years
ago when I had first seen Jon perform and how our paths had
finally crossed. That night the army of trucks, buses, and crew
headed off for Atlanta to begin setting up the next day's show. But
Jon stayed behind, along with guitarist Steve Howe, keyboardist
Igor Khoroshev, and several crew members. The next morning they
visited my farm and studio. We had a wonderful time listening to
music and talking over a barbecue. Jon recorded for a short time,
putting on a few final touches for an upcoming VH1 special. But all
too soon it was time for them to catch a plane to Atlanta for that
night's show.

Four months later my lifelong dream of making a record with
Jon Anderson came to pass when he and his wife, Jane, flew into
Nashville, where we spent six weeks writing and recording
together. For the first two weeks we wrote and sketched out ideas
for thirty songs! The following month we began to shape eleven
of those songs into our first CD. My daily routine consisted of
waking up, walking over to the studio, and recording with Jon.
Wow. I was living out what once was a distant dream. Besides
immersing ourselves in music, we spent hours in conversation,
sharing stories and developing a tight friendship. One of my
favorite memories is warming ourselves by the huge bonfires we
would build at night after a day of recording.

When our time was up, I drove them to the airport, where they
were to catch a flight to Canada to resume work on the next Yes
album, and I was thinking about how much I would miss them.
Jon and Jane had become part of our family. As I am putting the
final touches on this book, I am also daily continuing my work on

this album, finishing up my guitar parts, and adding other musicians to complete the sound of each song.

Every time the engineer runs a song down, there's Jon's voice and my guitar together, and I am reminded how wonderful things came from the risk I took by making a fool of myself to meet him. I'm also reminded of the power that can come from visualizing your dreams. Once you imprint a picture in your mind, your subconscious goes to work making it a reality. I've learned firsthand that opportunities are everywhere, but we must keep our eyes open. This experience has given me courage to look people in the eye and introduce myself, because you never know what friendships might develop, or what opportunities might arise.

When was the last time you sensed that an opportunity was nearby but you didn't have the courage to seize it? Maybe you saw the head of your company in a restaurant and you wanted to approach him or her and share your ideas, but you were afraid. Maybe you were sitting near someone interesting on an airplane but didn't have the courage to initiate a conversation. Perhaps you really hit it off with someone but didn't follow up. Or maybe you had the chance to mend a relationship, but you held back. Don't let your life be a series of missed opportunities. If you ever find yourself wondering whether or not to take a chance, the answer is undeniably and unquestionably — *yes!*

If you shy away from seizing an opportunity, you can be sure of what will happen: nothing.

Opportunities are everywhere, but only when we look for them with hopeful eyes will they appear.

CHAPTER SEVEN

BEATING THE ODDS

ew things are more fascinating than stories of people who beat the odds. I used to think that beating the odds was some kind of supernatural experience reserved for the chosen few. But I was wrong. Beating the odds is all about perseverance and persistence. It's about never giving up. If five people of equal talent are all going for the same goal, the person who hangs in there the longest will win out every time.

I'll even take things a step further. If one of those five people is slightly lacking in talent but makes up for it with their drive and determination, they will *still* win out over the others. Then there are those who not only have tremendous talent but they also have an equal amount of persistence and discipline. Tiger Woods is a great example of this type of person. And recently I saw a television special on Britney Spears. Until now I had viewed

Britney as a product of the "music industry machine," someone who had millions spent on her to wow the public with a lot of high-tech flash. But I was wrong again.

I should have known better. Since she was three years old she's been talking dancing, singing, and acting lessons. She became a Mouseketeer when she was ten. She's shown up for hundreds of auditions for commercials, Broadway shows, and recording contracts. She's won and lost on *Star Search.* Just before she signed with her current label, Jive Records, Sony and Mercury passed on her. Most interesting was that everyone interviewed said that while it was true that she had enormous talent as a dancer and a singer, she was also more focused and driven than anyone they had ever seen. Without all that determination she would have fallen into obscurity like thousands of other talented teenagers who have big dreams but lack perseverance.

RCA

Everything I had ever learned about perseverance was put to the test before I finally landed a major recording contract, but the payoff was well worth it. Walking down the Avenue of the Americas in New York City on the way to my first meeting as a signed artist with RCA's new imprint label Rendezvous Entertainment gave me a feeling of sheer ecstasy. It was incredible! In every direction was an endless sea of people scurrying about. There must have been thousands of musicians who had come to this city with the same dream I had.

I remember thinking to myself, "How did I get here? Why me? What did I do to deserve this? Was it because I had more talent?"

Of course not. I have always known scores of musicians who have more natural talent than I do. Was it luck? Hardly! I'd been preparing for this moment since my teens. I had been persevering for twenty years, slugging it out in every imaginable situation: sleazy clubs, county fairs, high school assemblies, and eventually hundreds of university campuses, living like a gypsy. There were those struggling years in Los Angeles. Even after moving to Nashville in search of sanity and a more balanced lifestyle, I was out of town most of the time — living a dream on the one hand and sacrificing everything on the other.

Like thousands of other aspiring musicians, I was in search of the holy grail of the music business: a record deal with a major label — Warner, Sony, MCA, Virgin, Arista. We all imagined getting a big recording contract followed by watching our songs rocket up the Billboard charts. Then we would film music videos destined for the Top 10 on MTV or VH1. If we could somehow land that elusive recording contract, big concert tours and all the other trappings of success would be sure to follow. This was our version of the American dream.

> *The quality of persistence is to the character of man*
> *As carbon is to steel.*
>
> **— Napoleon Hill**

Don't let me give you the wrong impression. Things were going along pretty well. Life was good. I had five national albums under my belt on smaller labels and was one of a select group of people who actually made a living performing concerts. My albums sold just enough to justify the next, and with each one I became more and more skilled. But I had never been able to land a major recording contract, which is what I needed for my career to lift off and fly.

Finally, I became so frustrated I swore to myself that I was going to land a deal no matter what it took. This was the turning point: when I made that conscious decision to become a major label artist *or bust!* This was when I first discovered that when a person truly commits to a goal, the *way* to achieve that goal will reveal itself. Most of us have to hit the wall before we finally reach deep down inside and find the strength to succeed. Although God gave each of us the tools to thrive, most of us never learn to use them.

Resolve *in advance* that no matter what happens, when the going gets rough you will never give up.

Successful people fail more than failures do. The difference is they keep getting back up until they succeed.

Once again, being the eternal optimist paid off. If I had known the odds of getting signed were about the same as winning the state lottery — or getting stru.ck by lightning on the way to buy a lottery ticket! — I might not have set my sights on such a career in the first place. But logic didn't play a big part in my decisions back then. So year after year I followed my heart, traveling thousands of miles to give concerts and spending hundreds of studio hours making records. Although I didn't realize it, I was doing exactly what I needed to beat the odds. Well, almost exactly; I still had to raise the bar a couple of notches higher before I was going to get noticed.

BEATING THE ODDS

When you get in a tight place and everything goes against you,
till it seems as though you could not hold on a minute longer,
never give up then, for that is just the time
and place the tide will turn.

— Harriet Beecher Stowe

BETTING EVERYTHING ON ONE SONG

Now that I had albums out, I thought the days of having to record demo tapes were over. But it was becoming obvious I needed to record new music that was more powerful than anything I had done before. So with the donated help of some of the finest musicians and engineers in Nashville, and after almost a year in the studio, I finally completed a demo tape I was thrilled with. After all that effort laboring over these new songs, I knew there was no turning back — no more excuses. It was time to lay it on the line.

In the past I would play my demo tapes for a few people, then quickly retreat after getting too much criticism. I allowed those rejections to undermine my confidence. The biggest obstacle in the way of my landing a major record contract was fear — I was paralyzed by it. I was paralyzed by fear of rejection, fear of failure, fear of pain, fear of the unknown, and finally, fear of success. At last I decided the only way I could deal with my fear was to face it head on, to look at it eye to eye and take action in spite of it.

The good news was that I had a new manager, Ken Mansfield, with an impressive track record, including working for the Beatles and managing Apple Records. He laid out a strategy that began with sending out thirty-five letters to record label executives, to be followed by a one-song cassette tape, if they replied with a request for it. The letter said, "I'm so positive I have a winner here, that listening to one song is all it will take." This bold, forceful approach landed us about a dozen requests for a tape. Unfortunately, everyone responded with a thumbs down. But Ken was not deterred. Next he mailed out fifty three-song tapes and once again... *not one positive response.*

My inclination was to call it quits. All this rejection was so painful. But Ken really believed in my music and assured me that many other artists who had gone on to great success had endured similar rejection. So we decided to give it one more try. We spent a few months regrouping, compiled a list of 137 record company executives, and sent each one of them a package including a revised tape of the same songs and at last, we got a couple of bites!

The first came from Arista, but soon we weren't getting return phone calls from them. We knew this was the kiss of death. Their excitement had obviously worn off, and nothing more was likely to happen. Then one Saturday afternoon Ken received a call from Jimmy Ienner, a major player in the music business. Not only did he love the tape, but the timing was perfect. He was the president of a new label called Rendezvous under the RCA umbrella, and he was searching for the right artists to sign. His resume read like a Who's Who in the music industry. Groups like Pink Floyd, Three Dog Night, Grand Funk Railroad, KISS, and Blood, Sweat and Tears are just a few of the acts he helped steer to great success.

Although my music was far more eclectic and avant-garde than that of other artists he'd worked with in the past, he considered that a positive. He was attracted to my multimedia stage show. He had seen how this approach had worked for Pink Floyd and believed the time was right to put the weight of his record company behind me. Almost immediately he put me in the studio. After five grueling months of recording seven days a week, we were done. A few months later *Electric Cinema* hit the streets. Overnight, my new record was in more than ten thousand stores and was being played on radio stations across the country.

Instantly new opportunities opened up. I was regularly appearing on national television and was invited to perform in bigger and more prestigious concert settings than ever before. Many other doors were opened to me that helped me to establish a more solid foundation under my career. In fact, having a record in the stores gave me the added credibility I needed to get a loan for my farm. It was such a great lesson, to witness what happens when I raised the bar and did whatever it took to get signed. All those new opportunities more than offset the rejection and pain I endured along the way. It was great!

You might say I just got lucky. You might say I was simply at the right place at the right time. I don't think so. Getting lucky happens by consistently trying and trying again until the odds are you'll be at the right place at the right time. Remember, one of the most important principles of success is persistence. Consider Thomas Edison, who experienced more than ten thousand failures before perfecting the incandescent lightbulb, or Walt Disney, who was turned down by 403 banks while trying to raise money to create Disneyland. If Ken and I had sent out only 136 tapes, maybe we would not have landed the deal. But through persistence we beat the odds.

Once you truly understand this concept, success will no longer seem like some mysterious or magical gift bestowed only on others. The best assets of everyone I know who has accomplished great things have been drive, determination, and persistence. This has certainly proved true in my case. Getting signed to RCA was one of the most challenging and gratifying experiences of my life. Although *Electric Cinema* never sold a million copies, it did produce a mild radio hit called "Sleepwalking," and the critics loved it.

Most important, landing this record deal gave me self-confidence to go out and do greater things with my life. It instilled in me the belief that anything is possible. That belief is more valuable to me than any financial reward.

Success comes to those who become success conscious.

— Napoleon Hill

No matter how overwhelming your quest, no matter how many "no's" you have to endure, remember that you only fail if you give up. People who are successful have had more failures than failures do, but the difference is they persevere and never quit. In my office I have a notebook containing *more than eighty letters of rejection* that preceded my long-awaited yes with RCA! I've included a few of those letters on the following pages. Take a moment to check them out, and take comfort in the fact that these are the kinds of rejections everyone braves before getting a yes! Let it serve as a reminder of how you too can beat the odds.

**There are no limits except the ones
you impose on yourself.**

**Your ability to persist even in the face of setbacks
and disappointments will determine where
you end up in the long run.**

Chrysalis Music Group

Chrysalis Music (ASCAP)
Chrysalis Songs (BMI)
9255 Sunset Boulevard, Suite 319
Los Angeles, California 90069-3498
Telephone: 310-550-0171

Fax: 310-281-8750

810 7th Avenue
New York, NY 10019
Telephone: 212-603-8769
Fax: 212-603-8759

8 April 1992

Chrysalis

Mr. Ken Mansfield
Front Row Management
2005 Convent Place
Nashville, Tennessee 37212

Dear Ken:

I'm sorry to have taken so long to respond to the Robin Crowe material. The sale, the move, new employees, etc. have kept me tied up with minutia rather than music.

At any rate, I've listened through a couple of times and asked my staff to do the same. Regretfully, we cannot muster enough enthusiasm, from a musical standpoint, to propell a deal through.

Please keep me informed on your other projects however, and I'll look forward to seeing you when you're next in Los Angeles.

Yours sincerely,

Tom Sturges
Senior Vice President and GM

TPS:dmr

JUMP AND THE NET WILL APPEAR

EMI
810 Seventh Avenue
New York, New York 10019
MICHAEL BARACKMAN
Vice President, A & R

September 26, 1990

Ken Mansfield
MAIN MANSFIELD ASSOCIATES
United Artists Tower
50 Music Square, Suite 200
Nashville, Tennessee 37203

Ken:

Oh boy. I noticed that I never had responded to you regarding Robin
Crow. This one totally fell through the cracks. I apologize profusel
It is embarrassing that you had sent me this so long ago without me
responding. There is no excuse.

For what it's worth, I did go through the package. I heard it more
for a New Age type of label a la Private Music. It wasn't really
something we could have sunk our teeth into. I did enjoy it (and woul
enjoy a CD if you have an extra one). Perhaps there is something more
mainstream-slanted that we can work together on.

I respect what you do, and would enjoy working together. I'll try to
hold up my end of the bargain in the future.

BEst,

Michael Barackman

MB/gl

MAIN MANSFIELD
A S S O C I A T E S

Ken
Good energy, but
I don't hear a breakthrough
hit single which might
launch the artist.
I'll have to pass.
RS

ay 15, 1991

rista Records
ichard Sweret
ix West 57th Street
ew York, NY 10019

ear Richard:

    A few months ago you expressed interest (after hearing
one song tape I sent you) on Robin Crow.

    So........here's five more new "monster" recordings which
e has just completed.

    Robin has been tearing up the college circuit with his
ntense stage show; and has developed quite a large following
ver the last few years. Let me know what you think---there
re more songs, press info., video, etc., if interested.

armest regards,

en Mansfield
resident

M/clc

nclosure

(ĭ·mä′gō

Ken Mansfield
Main Mansfield Assocs.
P.O. Box 50146
Nashville, TN37205

June 21st 1991

Dear Ken,

Thankyou for sending me the <u>Robin Crow</u> tape to listen to which we
have just been doing thismorning.

Getting straight to the point, I am really not a great fan of
'muso.' types of project - by which I mean where technique and
musical ability are the main attraction. Robin's playing (and the
production here) is very impressive, but it all sounds a bit
serious and bombastic for these ears. I really believe attitude and
great ideas are of paramount importance, over and above how
musically proficient an artist is. Also, this is really not the
type of artist Imago is looking to get involved with and develop.

Thus, I have to say that this is a pass. Robin seems to be the sort
of artist that Wyndham Hill or Elektra/Nonesuch might appreciate a
little more than I.

Thanks again, and good luck!

Sincerely,

Hugo Burnham
Director, A&R

CBS Records Inc.
1801 Century Park West
Los Angeles, California 90067-6406
(213) 556-4700

March 27, 1990

Mr. Ken Mansfield
Main Mansfield Associates
50 Music Square West, #200
Nashville, TN 37203

RE: ROBIN CROW

Dear Ken,

I've had a chance to review the enclosed materials
on Robin's music. It all sounds great and he's
an excellent guitar player but I don't feel that
Epic is the appropriate place for him. He belongs
on a label that can cater more closely to him and
his type of music. Labels that might be appropriate
for him include GRP, Restless and Guitar World's
new label.

I appreciate you keeping Epic in mind for Robin and
wish you luck in finding a home for him.

Regards,

Ken Komisar
Senior Director
West Coast A&R

KK:dac

enc.

MAIN MANSFIELD
A S S O C I A T E S

April 10, 1990

Dick Whitehouse
CURB RECORDS
3907 W. Alameda Avenue
7th Floor
Burbank, CA   91505

Dear Dick:

A quick hello!!

ROBIN CROW ??

Let me know!!

Warmest regards,

Ken Mansfield
President

KM/cg

4.23

Should I say "Let's Go!"?

I wish it were so because I think Mr. Crow spells "Dough" -- but only for those in the know ... (ie not us country type)

Suggest; Private Music, Narada, Nodus, or Windam Hill -- Michael Hedges notwithstanding.

Ken, This guy's great

Thanks

ANTIC
RDING
RATION

ANTIC

29
SSET
D.
GELES,
XX169

HONE:
05-7450
AX:
05-7475

April 21, 1991

Ken Mansfield
Main Mansfield Associates
P.O. Box 50146
Nashville, TN 37205

Dear Ken:

Thank you for submitting material to us. I found the tape
interesting, however, instrumental tracks are unfortunately
not what I am looking for at this moment. He did have an
ear-catching sound, though.

Please feel free to send any additional material that you may
have in the future.

Best Regards,

Kevin Williamson

KW:tob

ARISTA RECORDS, INC.
Arista Building
6 West 57th Street
New York, NY 10019
(212) 830-2252

MITCHELL COHEN
VICE PRESIDENT
A & R, EAST COAST

March 26, 1990

Ken Mansfield
Main Mansfield Associates
United Artists Tower
50 Music Square West
Suite 200
Nashville, TN 37203

Dear Ken:

I reviewed the video cassette you sent by Robin Crow, and althoug
he is a talented and creative guitarist, I really don't feel tha
his compositions or performances show breakthrough potential.
Since I don't hear the kind of distinctive musical qualities tha
would make a real impact, I'm going to pass on this porject, but
I appreciate your bringing Robin to Arista's attention.

Yours truly,

[signature: Mitchell Cohen]

MAIN MANSFIELD
A S S O C I A T E S

November 9, 1990

David Stamm
ARISTA RECORDS
Six West 57th Street
New York, NY   10019

Dear David:

Per your request I submit a more in-depth look at ROBIN CROW.
You asked for original material, so I have enclosed Robin's two
most recent CDs which include mainly his compositions.

The one song cassette of "The Wall" that sparked your interest in
Robin is more in the musical direction he would like to pursue at
this time.

Thanks for your interest. Enjoy, and I look forward to your response.

12-13

Warmest regards,

Ken —
He's a talented performer,
but the compositions and
overall concept don't strike me
as particularly compelling or unique.
So I'll have to pass on the
project for now. I do, however,
appreciate your sending the
material along.

Ken Mansfield
President

KM/cg

Enclosures

P.S. I have a video -- just ask!!

UNITED ARTISTS TOWER 50 MUSIC SQUARE WEST SUITE 200 NASHVILLE, TN 37203 (615) 329-2020 FAX - (615) 329-2081

JUMP AND THE NET WILL APPEAR

PolyGram Records™

••

May 16, 1990

Ken Mansfield
United Artists Tower
50 Music Square West, #200
Nashville, TN 37203

Dear Ken:

Sorry it's taken me so long to respond to Robin Crow, but I
finally got a chance to view his video. I was very impressed with
his guitar technique, but I feel he would be better served on a
label that specializes in New Age/Progressive rock type artists.
For this reason I am going to take a pass.

Again, I am sorry it's taken me so long to get back to you, and
if you come across any other exciting artists send them along.

Best wishes,

Tom Vickers

Tom Vickers
Director A&R
PolyGram/Wing Records

PolyGram Records, Inc.   Telephone: (818) 955-5200   Casablanca
3800 West Alameda Avenue   Fax: (818) 848-7530   Mercury
Suite 1500   Telex: 9104902149   Polydor
Burbank, CA 91505   PolyGram Classics
                                                                   Wing

CHAPTER EIGHT

ACHIEVING THE UNACHIEVABLE

The dreamers are the saviors of the world.
Composer, sculptor, painter, poet, prophet, sage,
these are the makers of the afterworld, the architects of heaven.
The world is beautiful because they lived;
without them, laboring humanity would perish.

— James Allen

After reading the last chapter you're probably saying to yourself, "That Robin sounds like a persistent guy." This is true. In fact perseverance and determination are essential to success. But this next chapter adds another key element. It's a trait that will make the difference in whatever you set out to do. It's the ability to consistently move forward toward your goals each and every day. It's the ability to follow through. It's the ability to take action even when you're unsure, to be willing to trust that your net *will* appear. This is where faith comes in.

This is the story of how I learned how powerful trusting and staying focused can be. Also this is the story of how I began building wealth. But more important, it is the story of how I overcame my self-perceived limitations — how, on a leap of faith and with $2,000, and a couple of sketches, I embarked on an enormous project that was to become my own enchanted castle: an eight-thousand-square-foot world-class recording facility constructed from hundreds of huge timbers, complete with horse stables, a fifty-foot lookout tower, multilevel lounges, guest rooms, and a state-of-the-art kitchen that looks up into a thirty-foot steeple!

When all was said and done, my dream studio, which started with $2,000 appraised for *more than $3,000,000!* But that's not how it started out. My dream didn't come true until the pressure became so great that I couldn't take it another day. That's when I found myself staring at two possibilities: either I was going to cave in and surrender to a life of mediocrity and just scraping by or I could rise up and face my fears straight on, learn what I was doing wrong, and begin to take charge of my destiny. My friend Brian Tracy says those who don't learn to set goals are doomed to work for those who do. Ouch! That was motivation enough for me.

$100,000 A YEAR — AND STILL BROKE

As I told you at the beginning of this book, after twenty years of hard work I had built a wonderful career. My albums were in stores nationwide, and each year I was performing between fifty and one hundred concerts, grossing more than six figures. Finally I began to ask the questions that had been lurking in the background but that I was afraid to face:

- Why was I almost always operating in the red?
- Why was I still living hand-to-mouth?
- Where did all the money go?
- Is this as good as it gets?

When I really began to look at my books, I realized that a one-person office to coordinate my concert schedule, a two-man road crew, constant upgrading of gear, massive overhead, and the endless assortment of managers, agents, accountants, lawyers, promoters, publicists, and investors were all costing more than I was making. It wasn't working. It was a financial black hole.

It was at about that time that I landed my deal with RCA. At last my wife, Nancy, and I were able to scrape together enough money to make a down payment on a small farm in Franklin, Tennessee, a few miles outside Nashville. Set among rolling hills, with a river running along one end, the property had a big log home constructed from four smaller cabins built in the 1830s. It was a bit drafty but had lots of atmosphere. After twenty years of waking up in a different city every day I finally had a place I could call home. At last we had a great place for raising our children and for building my long-desired home recording studio.

It turns out that my timing couldn't have been better, because my RCA album, *Electric Cinema*, wasn't selling well. You don't have to be a rocket scientist to figure out that big record companies expect big sales figures to offset their big investments. Believe it or not, some bands spend so much money recording and shooting videos that they won't break even unless their albums sell at least a million copies. Every year the recording scene seemed to be less about art and more about commerce.

The writing was on the wall. Unless I came up with some new music that had folks in New York turning back flips, I'd soon be dropped. So I put everything I owned — which consisted of my truck and touring gear — up for sale so that I could build my own recording studio — a place to create music without time limits. Then perhaps I could come up with the lightning in a bottle I needed to rejuvenate my record company's excitement in me...and if that didn't work maybe I'd be able to rent the place out and create some income.

There's a saying around Nashville: "How do you make a million dollars in the studio business? You spend two million on a studio." Everyone told me I was making a huge mistake, but that didn't slow me down. My studio was certainly not a million-dollar facility. In fact, it wasn't much more than a lean-to on the back corner of our house. But it was very professional and at the same time, it was unique and inviting. I simply created the kind of studio I had always wanted to record in. The whole place was filled with plants, skylights, and windows overlooking the countryside.

Once it was up and running, I called a few friends who produced records and suggested that they might enjoy renting the studio from time to time. I thought this would help offset expenses. Meanwhile I recorded night and day in hopes of cutting another album with RCA.

EXPECT the UNEXPECTED

How do you make God laugh? Just tell him your plans.

Before I knew it, I found my home studio turning into a business. Dark Horse Recording seemed like the perfect name for this business, because the dark horse is the unexpected winner, the long shot in a horse race. And the unexpected is just what happened. One by one people came out to record. And to my amazement people just loved the studio. I was not used to having success come my way so swiftly. Within a year and a half word of mouth had spread and pop stars like Neil Diamond, Martina McBride, and Faith Hill were cutting platinum-selling albums here. I had stumbled into the studio business!

But before the studio really took off, sure enough, I was dropped from RCA. I was about to turn forty, and Nancy was pregnant with our fourth child. Reality has really big teeth, and it bites! All of a sudden the truth was so obvious. I now had to somehow figure out how to make up for twenty years of making financial mistakes. I had spent so much of my life climbing up the ladder of success, but like I said before it was leaning against the wrong wall. There was so much I knew about the music business, but what did I know about the commitment it takes to becoming financially successful, to support a family?

I had so many questions: *Why did I feel so helpless? What was holding me back? Was I simply not smart enough to realize my dreams? Am I somehow trapped by my fears? Is there some way I can change? Can I have a successful career, wealth, and a rich family life? Is it possible to achieve these things while remaining spiritually balanced?*

These questions left me with a desire to do something unequivocal. What if I fixed my sights on a goal so big that I wouldn't have any time to open myself to negative influences? What if I let go, take a leap of faith, and trust the universe to light my way? What if...I expand my one small studio into a world-class studio complex?

Although I didn't know the answers, my gut told me to go for it...*to jump!* So I took out some notebook paper and began jotting down some ideas. I had absolutely no idea how I could raise the money, nor did I have a clue how much it would all cost, but I knew it was more money than I had ever seen before. My plan was simple...and naive. Just get started, I thought to myself. Somehow I'd work the rest out as I went along.

It's not until our backs are up against the wall that we discover what we're really capable of.

The word *impossible* is a smokescreen that blinds us from seeing our potential.

I BEGAN WITH ONLY $2,000

My first step was to hire someone with a bulldozer to clear a building site and reshape the hillside. At this point the building wasn't much more than a sketch on paper. It was to be 115 feet long, 65-five feet wide, and four stories tall! When the bulldozing was finished, I was already out of money. But the process had begun, and I now had a spot to stand on, to touch and feel. A place where I could visualize the next step. My neighbor Willie Anderson just happened to be an excellent barn builder by trade, and he was willing to help me now for compensation later. With the help of his two-man crew we began pouring footers and erecting the first level. My skills as a novice woodworker came in handy as well. For the next three years I put on a pair of overalls, rolled up my sleeves, and went to work. I put my musical aspirations on hold and worked on this building all my waking hours, sometimes for months at a time by myself. The scope of the project was so huge — relative to my limited financial resources — that in the beginning I didn't even tell my friends what I was up to for fear they would think I had lost my mind.

My first source of financing was to rob any income that Dark Horse Recording was bringing in. Then I began bartering studio time for outside labor. I took out lines of credit at several lumberyards. My goal was to find some way to keep moving things ahead each day. My plan was to build the studio with huge timbers and windows throughout, creating the effect of looking out from an enormous tree house. To realize that dream, I was going to need the help of a professional timber framing company, and a lot of money. Pioneer Log Homes came to the rescue. (This is when I began my education in qualifying for huge lines of credit from credit cards.) With their 70-foot crane they begin piecing hundreds of huge timbers into place like an enormous puzzle. It looked like an Amish barn raising, except for the crane, of course.

Opportunity is missed by most people because it is dressed in overalls and looks like work.

— Thomas Edison

A BUILDING WITH A LIFE OF ITS OWN

As the project grew, new possibilities came to light. The building began to take on a life of its own. A master craftsman named Stan Justice got involved early on. He was my "guardian carpenter," because no matter how impractical or outrageous my ideas were, he would always come up with a way to pull them off. With his guidance and can-do attitude we added a 54-foot-high lookout tower and a spectacular kitchen with a cathedral ceiling looking up into a 30-foot steeple, none of which was part of my original plan. Everyone thought I had gone mad. As far as I was concerned, I was simply going for it.

Often any decision is better than no decision at all.

The same thinking that got you where you *are* will rarely get you where you want to *be*.

As the design evolved, the floor plan became a maze of interesting twists and turns. There wasn't a square room or hallway in the entire building. It had two spiral staircases made from handnotched wooden beams. We built lookout decks on all sides, and installed 142 windows, providing outstanding views of the countryside from every room. When I got opinions from various contractors, I couldn't believe how inconsistent and conflicting they were, so it always came down to taking my best shot and making a decision myself. If there's one thing I've learned, it's the importance of making decisions and then taking action on them. Often any decision is better than no decision at all. Even if some of your choices turn out to be wrong, by doing this you will always be moving forward in the direction of your goals.

Early on I decided that my working time needed to be learning time. After all, the reason I started this project was to change my thinking and to improve my life. So I committed to listening to audio learning tapes night and day. I listened to tapes on business, achievement, time management, and leadership. I listened to tapes on spirituality, relationships, diet, and finding inner peace. The more I listened and learned, the stronger my confidence grew. For the first time in my life I began to understand that I was capable of realizing dreams that I once thought impossible. In fact, if not for the powerful coaching I received from these great thinkers, I don't think I would have had the courage to face many of the adversities that I came up against.

THE POWER OF FOLLOWING THROUGH

My most profound lesson was discovering the true power of following through. It's hard to stay enthusiastic when you work for weeks without seeing any visible progress. It's hard to be patient when the stacks of unpaid bills pile up. It's hard to stay excited when you don't know where you'll find the money to continue. But I knew I had no choice but to finish what I'd started. So every day I put one foot in front of the other and did my best to stay on track. In the bitter cold of winter and in the sweltering heat of summer I forged ahead. There were plenty of times when I just wanted to quit. But commitment to an idea is all about following through. So everyday that's what I did.

Meanwhile, the construction continued. It's exciting to plant a seed and watch it grow. At one point that's all this project was — an idea. Then it took on a life of its own. It had become such an enormous undertaking, unlike anything I had ever imagined. *Jump and the net will appear* became my mantra.

TAKING ONE STEP AT A TIME

Planning and organizing before starting a project is only common sense, yet I have seen instances where overplanning can lead to crippling procrastination. I always admire a well-thought-out and comprehensive business plan. But planning too much can become an excuse to avoid jumping. To accomplish anything it's essential to plan your course of action, but it means nothing unless you commit to follow through. That commitment will become the fuel to keep you going during hard times. It will give you the consistency and focus you need to keep moving forward one step at a time.

Always remember that achieving a large goal can only be accomplished by first breaking it down into smaller steps. Imagine you're preparing to drive cross-country from Los Angeles to Atlanta. It's only natural to mentally break the trip down into smaller parts. As someone who has traveled extensively, I can vouch for this. The thought of driving thousands of miles in one stretch is just too overwhelming. Say you're driving from Los Angeles to Atlanta. Visualize taking a break after 272 miles, which would land you in Las Vegas, perhaps taking time to catch a show or to try your luck at the tables for a few hours. Now, rejuvenated, move on to Flagstaff, and then perhaps Albuquerque, and so on, until, before you know it, you're on the home stretch to Atlanta. There's no way I could have completed this new studio without breaking the process down into a thousand small steps, each one doable on its own.

> *Impossibility: a word only to be found*
> *in the dictionary of fools.*
>
> — **Napoleon Bonaparte**

We were now three years into the project. Some days it seemed like it would never end. But on others I could glimpse the light at the end of the tunnel, and I was thrilled. Every window and door was in, all the interior walls were up, the electricity was on, and now we were ready to begin trimming out the inside. It was at this time that I met Ted Judy, a world-class trim carpenter who also happened to be an accomplished singer-songwriter. More than fifty carpenters had worked on some part of this building, but none was more gifted or took more pride in their work than Ted. He went to work building cabinetry and trimming out each of the thirty-eight rooms in the building. That was more than four years ago, and Ted has been working here ever since. Every day for the three and a half years we've been open, Ted has continued to transform Dark Horse Recording into a work of art. Day after day, room after room, his endless attention to detail has made our studio a feast for the eyes from ceiling to floor.

One of the secrets of our success at Dark Horse is a simple philosophy: "Make money now — organize later." I know entrepreneurs who spend so much of their energy and money to present a professional front. The entire dot-com industry was built using this approach. There are those who won't even make that first phone call until everything's perfectly set up and in place. This approach has been the death of many young business start-ups. The truth is, things are rarely just right. Your success in business will always be in direct proportion to your ability to take action.

THE CREDIT CARD GAME

By now you're probably saying, "This is all well and good, but how did you come up with the money?" Good question! The answer is a thousand different ways. It's amazing how creative you can be when you've laid it all on the line. My family sacrificed in every area of our lives. We cut expenses to the bone. We took on the mind-set that having a big goal was an adventure, that it would be exciting to work on it together and see it through. We sold our best car, leaving only one for a family of six. (You know, it wasn't even that big of a sacrifice.) We took no vacations, rarely went out to eat, and committed ourselves to spending as little as possible on things like clothes and furniture. Let's be honest here. As a culture we're spoiled rotten. None of these sacrifices brought us unhappiness or stress. In fact, they gave us a sense of unity, mission, and love.

But sacrificing material pleasures only got us a small fraction of the way. Cutting back and selling things gave us about a $30,000 jumpstart, but that was it. Then it was time to get down to the business of finding real money. My next move wasn't very creative and it's one I wouldn't recommend. In fact, it bordered on financial suicide. You guessed it: credit cards!

In my defense I will say that I had always been very disciplined with them in the past, but that was about to change. I believed with all my heart this venture was worth the risk, so I was willing to take some chances. What I did was not for the weak of heart: I ran up $84,000 on the cards in three months! That comes to almost $115,000, enough to make a pretty big dent in the initial framing, but that's all.

A man cannot directly choose his circumstances,
but he can choose his thoughts, and so indirectly,
yet surely, shape his circumstances.

— James Allen

LANDING A LOAN

My next step was to secure real financing and pay back those credit cards. This meant dealing with banks, and I would rather have had a root canal. Before getting a mortgage on my farm, I had never been able to secure a loan for even $500. Even though my credit was flawless, I was a self-employed musician. In the banking world, that's one level up from an ex-con! I used to make up jokes to compensate for my homespun accounting practices. After all, filling out all those applications was intimidating. It all seemed so painful, that I wouldn't even apply for loans in the first place.

But slowly I began to learn how the banking system operates, how to impress loan officers, and how their formulas work. I also learned that all banks are not created equal. There are people out there who *will* look beyond the numbers and take an interest in your character, intent, and accomplishments. So after tremendous struggle and countless rejections, I found a banker who was willing to color outside the lines and give me a loan. It turns out that after three years of continual improvements the value of my property had quadrupled! Aha! This was a very interesting concept, a formula I could repeat called refinancing! Building up a piece of property was something I clearly knew how to do, and it was something bankers could relate to. All that those banks were basically saying was... "Show me the collateral and I'll show you the money!" No problem!

Once the money came through, the first thing I did was pay off my credit cards, leaving me with just under $100,000 with which to breathe new life into the project. Landing that first loan was a defining moment for me. I knew if I could do it once, I could do it again. It wasn't long before I had to put that statement to the test. My initial loan provided just enough funds to complete things halfway. It was like climbing a huge mountain. Now that I could see the top I was more determined than ever to keep going.

Six months later I had again depleted my money. By this time I was becoming a Jedi Master at playing the credit card game. Because I had recently paid off all my cards, I was barraged with new credit card offers. As nerve-racking as it was, once again I began running them up. It was the only way I could keep things moving. With my increased line of credit I had plenty of rope with which to hang myself. This time I ran my cards up to $134,000! I carefully reviewed every offer in order to get the lowest introductory rates. It got so complicated that I made up charts and graphs tracking the rise and fall of all those wonderful introductory offers. You know how it works: at first they tempt you with 3.9 percent; then after six months the rate shoots back up to 20 percent. This is how credit card companies lure people in and then go for the kill. My goal was to beat them at their own game.

**Neither genius nor talent
can take the place of persistence.**

**Success is never an accident:
It's a direct result of your willingness to stay focused
and follow through.**

At this point my overhead was sky high. My only income came from my small studio. I had run up lines of credit with everyone, and these enormous payments were due each month as I was still looking for money to push the project ahead. The risk was getting greater by the day. It was becoming painfully obvious that if wasn't careful I could ruin my family financially.

Once again I was hunting for a mortgage company that would refinance my property. I figured that in the year since my first refinancing, my property had at least doubled in value. Why?

Because I was buying materials from salvage yards, because I was the contractor, because I was the main carpenter, and because I had lots of help from my friends. For every dollar I put in, the property would appraise for three more. Remember success comes disguised as overalls and long hours. Very few high achieving people get around this universal fact. There I was, back on the streets in search of a lender who was also a believer in my mission. Would you believe I had to go through this entire process two more times before I was finished? It's true!

Like so many journeys in life, had I known how far I'd have to travel, I probably would never have started. That's when the human spirit triumphs. That's when we learn who we really are — and who we can become. I learned to walk into a bank with the confidence that I could talk intelligently about finances. Now I can ask for a million-dollar loan and respond to the countless questions with intelligent answers. In fact, I can even get them to say yes! It was another six months before the building was finished enough to begin installing all the studio equipment. Four months after that we were ready to make music. It had been three years and three months from the day I brought in that bulldozer to the day we fired up the studio and began recording.

WITH A LITTLE HELP FROM MY FRIENDS

There is no such thing as a self-made man.
You will reach your goals only with the help of others.

— George Shinn

I could never have gotten this project off the ground, let alone have finished it, without help from my family and countless friends. But my enthusiasm attracted helping hands from some unlikely places. I learned that people want to be a part of something extraordinary. Neighbors would come over to help lift beams into place. My friends and family helped on weekends to paint or clean up the job site. My two teenaged boys, Andrew and Joseph, put in countless hours helping me, and I know the memory of what we accomplished together will be a lifelong reminder of what they are capable of.

More than once my parents bailed me out when I painted myself into a financial corner. For instance, about eighteen months into the construction, as the project headed into its second winter, it started raining every other day. The building's framework was up and the roof was ready to be shingled, but only half the outside walls and windows were in. Whenever a rainstorm hit, the building took a real beating. My folks came to the rescue. Many times over the years they've lent me money, but this time they presented me with a gift — enough money to pay for getting the roof shingled and the building dried in.

There's a fine line between having faith that things will work out and putting others under pressure to help you. It's definitely a line you don't want to cross very often. Having said that, there is no greater sense of unity and satisfaction than when people band together to pursue a worthy goal.

IF YOU BUILD IT, THEY WILL COME

Since the day we turned on the recording equipment in our four-studio complex, the phone has been ringing with people requesting recording time. The very first month we were open my studio income tripled! Four years later Dark Horse Recording is a thriving business that brings in a steady income, whether I'm there or not. Why? I believe that all the effort we put into this project has made us stand out from the crowd. There is nothing usual about this extraordinary sanctuary in the country, and people are attracted to that. We opened our doors without any fanfare. Word of mouth began to spread, and now we have become a haven for many of the biggest stars in the world.

With any large project it's easy to go through periods of wanting to throw in the towel and settling for less than what we had hoped to achieve. But remember, the race always goes to those who endure in the long run. True victory is about perseverance, determination, and never giving up. When I was in the middle of this project, I was exhausted from working on it sometimes a hundred hours a week, and I was tired of being turned down by so many banks. To make matters worse, the studio business had taken a downward turn because of sagging sales in the country music industry. At the same time, a dozen new studios were being built in the Franklin area alone.

But I was already in motion. I knew that if I didn't get the money, successfully finish the studio, and overcome all those obstacles, it would mean bankruptcy for me and my family. That was a powerful incentive for finding a way to succeed. Every day I found a reason to keep going, and when it was complete I had something I could really be proud of.

Remember that the benefits of accomplishing a worthy goal are always greater than just making a profit or checking another achievement off your to-do list. Achieving something big gives you confidence and strength of character, helping you to far exceed your self-imposed limitations. Sometimes taking risks comes down to a spiritual feeling that's deeper than logic or reason. We live in a society where people can get crushed by a system that doesn't always support individuality or creativity. We are taught very early to conform and to be normal, yet many who have accomplished extraordinary things were misfits. Somehow they persevered. Whether your goal is large or small, whether it's mainstream or on the fringe, it started with your idea. That's what Dark Horse Recording is — an idea realized. And it became real because I made a decision to take action. It got built because I decided to build it! When all is said and done, the dreams you make real will be those you decide to make real.

CHAPTER NINE

EXPANDING ᴏᴜʀ CIRCLE ᴏF POSSIBILITIES

As you sit reading this book someone is climbing Mt. Everest, a couple is sailing around the world in a sailboat, a woman is skydiving for the first time. They all are pushing against their comfort zone, becoming stronger, more confident, and less afraid. Climbing mountains and crossing oceans are big accomplishments, but every time we push ourselves, even with little tasks and small steps, we grow stronger.

It may sound like a cliché, but there is nothing more inspiring than the power of the human spirit. Even when it seems like we're not going to make it another step, that spirit survives. There are no limits to how high the human spirit can soar. It has motivated humankind to triumph in the face of despair and hopelessness. It has brought us from the Dark Ages to the Computer Age. People like Henry Ford, Amelia Earhart, Walt Disney, Madame Curie, Rosa Parks, and Bill Gates are just a few of the people who have changed our lives forever by pushing the edge. They are patron saints of the impossible. They took on challenges that seemed unfeasible — even harebrained — and went on to achieve extraordinary results.

The good news is that the rest of us mere mortals can do this as well. All of us can gauge our personal progress, not against others, but against ourselves — against our own self-imposed limitations. Remember, we can't compare our own boundaries to anyone else's. No one's pursuit of personal excellence is insignificant. How could it be, when our lives are such beautiful works of art, something only God could create? There are literally thousands of examples of how the human spirit is constantly finding ways to ascend to higher states of excellence.

SEVEN HUNDRED MILES IN ELEVEN HOURS

Okay, you're right, here comes another one of my road stories. You're probably saying, "Big deal. I've driven seven hundred miles in eleven hours once or twice." Do I think this small accomplishment somehow compares with Lee Iacocca turning Chrysler around or Tiger Woods winning the Masters Gold Tournament by twelve strokes or Sarah Hughes winning the gold medal in figure skating at age sixteen? Of course not. But there's more to my story than simply driving hundreds of miles on the interstate. The reason I'm telling you this story is to make one simple but important point. By widening our circle of possibilities, each one of us can take our lives to a higher place. What we do doesn't have to be profound or grand, as long as it challenges our capabilities.

In the early 1990s, I was still touring the college circuit, but now I was traveling with six thousand pounds of gear, a two-man crew, and a bigger truck. I was only spending about 125 days a year on the road, the concerts were in nicer venues, and the crowds were larger. Now I was traveling in a 1980 former Ryder truck, not unlike the 1964 former U-Haul I drove in earlier years. Just as before, I converted the front section into a camper. It obviously didn't compare to those plush tour buses that big-time acts travel in, but it was mine and it was paid for. I put so many miles on it, that in eight years I had to replace the engine three times! My two-man crew was in charge of setting up the three tons of sound and lighting equipment we carried from city to city. If you think that sounds like a romantic job, think again.

A DAY ON THE ROAD

After driving hundreds of miles, most often through the night, we would arrive at the concert site, usually a college auditorium or student center. On a typical day we would arrive around noon. After a brief bite to eat we would jump into action. My crew, along with a dozen volunteers, would begin unloading all our lights and speakers, rear screen projectors, guitars, and other gear and get it positioned on the stage. They had it down to a science. With military precision they would systematically unload the sixty-five road cases we carried, and like a giant puzzle, piece by piece assemble our beautiful stage production. They would wire up the 130 lights placed on overhead trusses and on 20-foot-high scaffold towers. They would equalize the speakers to the acoustical idiosyncrasies of each auditorium. They would focus projectors, aim the lights, and tune the guitars. Every cable had to be taped down, every sound and light setting triple-checked. And it all had to ready one hour before show time. As in life, each show's success was largely the sum total of countless details.

Meanwhile, I'd be out promoting. Sometimes I'd do a local radio or TV interview. But more often than not my promotional campaign consisted of walking through student centers and cafeterias, going table to table, handing out flyers, and inviting everyone to the concert. It may not sound glamorous, but it was effective, and the student activities director (that's who writes the check) was always pleased. All this self-promoting was humbling and at times even humiliating, but it produced results. It was something other performers weren't willing to do, so it gave me a competitive edge.

In order to have a rainbow,
you have to put up with a little rain.

— **Dolly Parton**

The real test was up to me. The audience wasn't interested in whether I had a good or bad day. They didn't care if I had a headache or the flu. So often I'd perform on two or three hours of sleep, but that's part of the challenge of life on the road. You rise to the occasion and give it your best. You give more than is expected.

Well, all good things must come to an end. In a flash the show would be over, and we'd have to reverse the whole process. What took six hours to erect was undone in just an hour and a half. Once the truck was loaded, we wasted no time heading toward the next day's destination. It was not uncommon to travel five or six hundred miles overnight between concerts. Each of us would take our turn at the wheel while the others slept in the back. And

sometimes we repeated this four or five days in a row before slowing down to catch our breath. It wasn't glamorous, no one was
making a fortune, it bordered on abuse, and we loved it!

**If you don't believe in achieving the impossible you won't
be able to achieve the extraordinary.**

**Always focus on producing results over creating activities
that look good but don't get you closer to your goals.**

THE CHALLENGE

It was the middle of February, so naturally we were touring up
north. The three of us were in the middle of a ten-day run, playing our last concert at the University of Minnesota in Morris. At
the last minute my office manager, Cheri Cline, uncovered a possible "pick-up" concert at Maryville College in St. Louis to be performed the day after the Minnesota concert. The catch was the
concert had to start at noon. We knew we would be driving right
through St. Louis just a half-day later on our trip home anyway. It
seemed a shame that we couldn't somehow find a way to make
it work. So we put our heads together to see if it was doable.

Not only was it a 700-mile trek, but there were no direct inter-
states or highways connecting these two cities — nothing but
zigzagging country highways adding mileage and slowing us
down. After factoring in the fastest possible stage strike in Morris,
and the leanest, meanest setup in St. Louis, we realized we had
fewer than eleven hours to get there. Although common sense was
not on our side, the lure of everyone earning an extra day's pay
clinched it. We just had to try!

The afternoon before our University of Minnesota concert we began to plot out our complex route, cutting back and forth on county roads and two-lane state highways. We figured if we averaged seventy miles per hour, didn't miss a turn, and the truck ran perfectly, we had an outside chance of arriving in St. Louis by 11:00 A.M. That would leave us an hour to unload the truck and set up a stripped-down set up of only guitars and sound — all we needed for the outdoor show. Normally we'd average about forty-five miles per hour, including stops. We had to figure a way to increase that average to seventy!

It's amazing how creative you can become when you're put to the test. First we made a list of every timesaving solution we could think of. Then we gathered our local college stage crew together and explained that we had to somehow load up the truck in just thirty minutes instead of the usual ninety. Everyone was up for the challenge; in fact, it became a fun competition with the clock to see if we could pull it off. As the stage went up that afternoon, my crew carefully explained to each stagehand how every piece of equipment would be packed up and loaded later that evening. We assigned each person a detailed list of tasks to accomplish at the show's end. We literally put them in charge, trusting that we could rely on them to help us make it.

My crew and I had always thought we were organized, but now we had raised the bar. As the concert ended, everyone sprang into action. I wish you could have been there. Those students, along with my crew, were like a crack team of experts swiftly tearing down, packing, and loading all six thousand pounds of equipment in just over thirty minutes. We were on our way.

But that was just the beginning. We turned every gas refill into a pit stop. One person would pump gas, while another would check under the hood, and another would pay. Besides having a designated driver, we also had a designated navigator as we continuously debated all our complex routing options during our night ride across the country. We challenged ourselves not to waste a single minute. We were so wired by the challenge that none of us slept a wink all night.

And guess what? We made it! That night we drove just over seven hundred miles in eleven hours without sleep, and, under the worst road conditions imaginable, we showed up at Maryville College fifteen minutes before show time! With the help of a few dozen students who muscled my gear onto the stage, we pulled off that afternoon concert without a hitch — other than starting about a half hour late. Then within a few hours we were headed home to Nashville, ahead of the original schedule we had set up before our St. Louis challenge. We were sleepy but ecstatic!

The fact that I earned extra money was negligible compared to the lesson I learned about overcoming perceived limitations. By pushing ourselves to the edge we learned how much more we were capable of. We had thought we were working hard and running an efficient operation, but after this, driving five or six hundred miles a day between shows became a breeze. This is exactly how athletes in training stretch their limitations; they continually push themselves to the next level. What once seemed overwhelming becomes commonplace. Remember, just as a runner might constantly push himself to higher levels, we can all do the same in every area of our lives. As we raise our standards of excellence in our relationships, in our health, in our faith, and in our careers we are shaping our destiny. We will create an extraordinary quality of life.

Trusting and relying on others is one of the best ways
to motivate people to do their best.

Pushing yourself to the edge might help you
achieve more, earn more, or do more,
and the lessons you'll learn will be priceless.

CHAPTER TEN

LIVING AN ABUNDANT LIFE

Neither a lofty degree of intelligence
nor imagination nor both together go
to the making of genius.
Love, love, love, that is the soul of genius.

— Wolfgang Amadeus Mozart

In the introduction to this book I suggested that we redefine what success means to each of us. In the next two chapters I will focus on the spiritual side of our quest to realize our dreams. In one way or another we're all seeking ways to find happiness and fulfillment. And we all know that success alone doesn't bring happiness.

Mother Teresa said that the greatest poverty was spiritual, not physical. It's easy to measure our material wealth, but to gauge spiritual wealth we have to look at our lives as a whole. How do we value our life and the lives of others? What are the depths of our relationships? Have we used our gifts for the good of others as well as ourselves? How well do we love? Happiness is not a by-product of circumstances, but rather a spiritual place we can tap into regardless of our circumstances.

LOOKING WITHIN

Our culture teaches us constantly to raise our standards for happiness. It's partially human nature, but our focus on material things makes matters a lot worse. Hundreds of times every day we are bombarded with advertisers telling us that if we wear the right clothes, use the right shampoo, drive the right car, or associate with the right people we will be happy.

When we buy our first 15-inch-screen television, we feel good for a while. Over time we discover that it no longer satisfies our demand for quality; we have now raised our standards for what is acceptable. So we set our sights on a bigger and more expensive television that meets our current definition of acceptable. This time it's a 27-inch set with a better picture and sound. For a while it seems like this is as good as it gets. But then we start asking ourselves, "What if I had a high-definition big-screen television? What if I had a DVD player? What if I had a surround-sound system?" For a while we're satisfied until we started thinking we need one for the bedroom and begin the process all over again. It's a trap. These things may provide a brief illusion of contentment, a sense of comfort and security, but they will never bring lasting happiness.

LIVING AN ABUNDANT LIFE

It is second nature to thirst for a full and rewarding life, but we often look in the wrong places. If our quest for material wealth is based on what we can get instead of what we can give, then we will be left empty. What happens after the high has worn off from the things we buy? We must look within ourselves, not outside to TVs and cars and gadgets, for real happiness. For only when we learn to change our inner world does our outer world also begin to change.

Happiness is not a state to arrive at but, rather,
a manner of traveling.

— **Samuel Johnson**

We have all sorts of ideas about what will make us happy. What will it take? Winning the lottery? Being admired by others? Becoming a millionaire? Riding the perfect wave? Performing the perfect concert? These might be worthy endeavors, but when you think it through it becomes clear that they will never bring the kind of lifelong happiness we desire — a rich, fulfilling satisfaction through good times and bad.

But, Robin, you ask, what about a those six-thousand-square-foot custom homes or those romantic vacations in Tahiti? What about sending our children to the best colleges? What about a solid financial foundation built on an impressive investment portfolio? Are you telling me I can't have those things and be happy? You already know part of the answer.

You can certainly find happiness with — or without — those things, but they will never make you happy by themselves. From what I've seen both in my own life and in the lives of people around me, when you become wealthy whatever traits you have will simply be intensified. If you are an angry person without money, you will become even angrier with money when things don't go your way. If you are generous when you have very little, then you will be very generous when you have a lot.

Learning how to love and become someone who can be loved is the most important path we can travel.

When we stay focused on our Higher Calling, all the challenges and hardships we experience become part of a greater spiritual quest.

Looking back on the last twenty years of touring, I figure I've driven more than a million miles. All this travel time has given me a lot of time to ponder the question of happiness. I've met all kinds of people — rich and poor, young and old. After all those miles and all those encounters, it's so obvious to me that lasting happiness never comes from outside circumstances — like making money, finding romance, becoming famous, or gaining power.

THIS MUST BE HEAVEN

It's really the *striving* and the *doing* that brings much of our happiness. Years ago I saw an old episode of *The Twilight Zone*. To this day I've never forgotten this crazy tale about a man I'll call Grant who had just died and gone on to some kind of afterlife. He found himself in a fabulous penthouse suite surrounded by beautiful furniture, art, and women who waited on him hand and foot.

They laid about stroking his hair and feeding him fruit. (Remember, this was the early sixties.) He found he had amazing talent as a virtuoso pianist. He was clever and witty. Everyone laughed at his jokes. Grant won every game of cards, and when he played pool he made absolutely every shot, no matter how difficult. As he looked around at his new surroundings, his tailor-made clothes, the priceless art hanging on the walls, he said to himself, "This must be heaven."

When one door of happiness closes, another opens;
but often we look so long at the closed door
that we do not see the one that has been opened for us.

— Helen Keller

Another man hovered in the background, acting as Grant's host, assisting him and heeding his every request. Grant told him how proud he was to have ended up in this nirvana. It was just the way he always knew it would be. He could indulge his fantasies in this perfect world where nothing could go wrong. He was in a constant state of bliss.

Yet, as you might guess, something wasn't quite right. He could not put his finger on it, but soon his pleasures began to sour. Surely this is what happiness is all about, he told himself. Yet happiness eluded him. He began to remember his past, thinking nostalgically about his old life. He actually began to miss its challenges and adversities. At last Grant said to his host, "Maybe this heaven is not for me. I'm more suited for a bit of struggle and strife. Perhaps I should give the other side a try." His host looked him in the eye and said, "Well, my friend, you're already there. *This is hell.*" No adversities to overcome. No challenges to face. We dream of it. We want it. But it wouldn't make us happy.

TRUE SUCCESS

The most important message I wish to convey is this: *True* success, the kind that leads to real happiness, is measured by who we become as people. Here's a story to make my point: Christmas is big deal in our family. My children spend months anticipating how much fun they're going to have and, of course, what great new gifts they might receive. Nancy and I try to plan ahead, because we have so many relatives and friends to think about, not to mention our four children. We have five people on staff, plus ten or so interns to think about as well. On top of all that I try to mail out gifts to some clients whom I also consider to be friends. Two Christmases ago I picked thirty-two people who fit that description. Some of those people I hadn't seen for a while, and others I see almost every week.

When Christmas is over I confess that I'm not very good at writing thank-you letters — partly because I've never learned the art of writing a short but sweet thank you. My other excuse is that I'm always too busy. Both my excuses are lame. But I tell you this to make a point: out of the thirty-two people whom I sent gifts, I received two thank you letters. Here's the irony: the two people who took the time to write and say thanks are perhaps the two busiest of the thirty-two. They're the two to who have more demands on their time and who have the most intense schedules. Ironically, they are also the most famous of the thirty-two. The two people that wrote thank-you letters to me are not people I see very frequently. I believe they wrote those thank-you letters because they are in the habit of going the extra mile for others. They know that small gestures go a long way.

Those two people were Dolly Parton and Naomi Judd. This is not to say that the others where the least bit rude; they are all friends whom I like and respect. Plus, I hadn't sent them the gifts expecting anything in return. They were simply sent in the spirit of Christmas. But having said that, those two letters got me thinking about who Dolly and Naomi are as people. Their small acts of courtesy and thoughtfulness go hand in hand with why they are so successful with their careers and why they're so successful as people. It was a great reality check for me. They've inspired me to step up and be more giving to others. It also got me thinking how small acts of kindness can make other people feel so good. You never know how important a little positive reinforcement can be to someone.

I can live for two months on a good compliment.

— Mark Twain

Happiness is not a by-product of circumstances, but rather a spiritual place we can tap into at any time.

Once we cultivate an attitude of gratefulness, then we naturally begin to look beyond ourselves to the needs of others.

If you help people get what they want,
then they'll help you get what you want.

— Zig Ziglar

You can't always get what you want,
But sometimes you just might find,
you get what you need.

— Mick Jagger

LOVE AND SUCCESS

We all need to be loved. When I first struck out on my own I was determined to show my parents and my friends a thing or two. Subconsciously I was thinking, "When I become a big rock star, then they'll love me more!" In fact, I believed that when I became rich and famous *everyone* would love me. During my twenties that thought pattern became the driving force in my life. It became my identity. My people skills left a lot to be desired, so I looked to my musical abilities to somehow fill in and bring love to my door.

This approach is filled with flaws, of course. It kept me from looking at what kind of person I really was or at my need to become a better person. Instead my obsession with musical success escalated as I threw myself into my work. Now this in and of itself isn't a bad thing. To have a burning desire to succeed in something is one of the most fundamental keys to success. The irony is, if we don't learn how to love and become someone who can be loved, then we're missing the entire point.

If I have the gift of prophecy and can fathom
all mysteries and all knowledge,

and if I have a faith that can move mountains,
but have not love, I am nothing.
If I give all I possess to the poor
and surrender my body to the flames,
but have not love, I gain nothing.

— 1 Corinthians 13:2

How many times have we heard stories about famous people who seemed to have everything going for them, yet whose lives spun totally out of control — sometimes even driving them to suicide? A person can easily spend years striving for success for all the wrong reasons. When I was in my twenties the driving force behind my desire to be a guitarist was the need to draw attention to myself. I believed that attention would lead to love and that would lead to happiness. It was a totally flawed plan, yet so many people live their lives using just that blueprint. They work and work so that they will be loved, yet they have no time for love!

If you achieve great wealth at the expense of your health, what do you have?

If you acquire power and fame, yet you never see your children, what do you have?

If your career becomes more important than your wife or husband, what do you have?

Wouldn't you rather be broke and have a house full of love than have lots of money and no love? A house without love has no foundation. It's just a matter of time until the wind begins to blow and it all comes crashing down. If you fill your heart with love for others, that love becomes the foundation you build on, and it's a foundation of solid rock.

To love for the sake of being loved is human,
but to love for the sake of loving is angelic.

— Alphonse De Lamartine

Jesus was right! "Many who are first shall be last and many who are last will be first." "It is better to give than receive." "The meek shall inherit the earth." These paradoxical statements seem simple enough, but are hard words to swallow when we're trying to get ahead in life. We put all our energy into striving for a better life, but why are we so unhappy and discontent with life in the fast lane — or the *me* lane?

Familiar acts are beautiful through love.

— Percy Bysshe Shelley

It's one of the universal laws of life: Before we receive love, we must give love. Before we receive a smile we must give a smile. Before we can receive a blessing we must give a blessing. Jesus said it another way: "He who sows sparingly shall reap sparingly, and he who sows generously shall reap generously." This scripture reminds us of the law of giving and receiving. When we believe our lives are filled with abundance and prosperity, then we will *know* abundance and prosperity. But again, in order to receive abundantly we must give abundantly. When we learn to be truly generous, we find ourselves being swept along in the flow of abundance. So often people live with a mind-set of scarcity; they become fearful. This stops them cold in their tracks when it comes to expending energy to help others. I know so many people just like that. Our culture provides us all with so many images of scarcity. Thoughts of running out of food or out of fuel or of the economy going under bring fear into everyone's minds.

Think about it. God wouldn't have allowed our planet to be populated with billions and yet deny them the ability to feed and shelter themselves. Nor would God have created a world in which one person's gain would be another's loss. I believe the resources we need are here in abundance if we are willing to cultivate an attitude of trust. Spiritual abundance is always about letting go. The irony is that having a belief in scarcity is always about holding on out of fear. That's when we get caught up in a vicious circle that becomes so hard for us to break: the more fearful we are, the harder we hold on, and the harder we hold on, the more fearful we become. But once we do break through to a belief in unlimited bounty then we let go and enjoy more abundance than we ever dreamed was possible.

SPIRITUALITY AND SUCCESS

"No one can serve two masters," Jesus said in the book of Matthew. "Either he will hate one and love the other, or he will be devoted to the one and despise the other. You cannot serve both God and Money." So many people grapple with the issue of balancing spirituality and materialism. At first glance it seems that focusing on building wealth would be at a tremendous cost to one's soul.

On the other hand, focusing on spiritual matters only would lead to poverty, especially if you are called on to be a provider. This issue really hits home with me. All four of my children are in private school. Does this mean I'm doomed to a life of spiritual poverty because every day I must focus on the bottom line? I don't think so. Do you think Jesus is saying we should escape into our own selfish worlds of spirituality and forsake the responsibilities that have been entrusted to us? Of course not! I have always believed that separating spirituality from the rest of our lives is like shooting ourselves in the foot. Our personal relationship with God is what gives us the inner strength to create a life of excellence and abundance.

Remember that your business life and your spiritual life should go hand in hand. Your spiritual life should be reflected in the way you run your business, the way you treat those with whom you work, and the way you treat your competitors. Honor, honesty, and integrity are essential ingredients in spiritual and material abundance.

As the Blues Bothers used to say, "I'm on a mission from God!" I believe that providing for and raising my family is my spiritual calling. When I stay focused on that fact I find my balance. If you stay focused on your Higher Calling, all the hard work and adversity becomes part of a greater spiritual quest. (I will discuss this at greater length in the next chapter.) Financial success and spirituality directly support each other when we direct our thoughts and actions appropriately. Once we begin to cultivate an attitude of continual thankfulness and gratitude, we naturally begin to look beyond ourselves and become more aware of the needs of others.

A grateful heart will bring you riches from within. If you have gratitude, you are like a bright light shining the way for others to follow. This attitude in turn leads to successful relationships, successful parenting, and successful careers. With a grateful heart you'll be successful in influencing others, and more important, you'll be successful in influencing yourself. The obstacles that hold us back from succeeding are always internal. The key to unlocking our unlimited potential is the ability to master our emotional state. Success and spirituality are completely intertwined, yet most people compartmentalize their walk with God and their idea of a successful career. But it's all part of the same picture. All the shapes and colors complement one another.

Remember, happiness doesn't depend upon who you are or what you have; it depends solely upon what you think.

— **Dale Carnegie**

Over the years my definition of success has dramatically changed. Wouldn't you agree that we tend to admire people who are

- willing to sacrifice for others
- willing to go the extra mile
- trustworthy
- dependable
- passionate
- cheerful
- positive
- courageous
- fearless
- honest?

So when you think about what makes someone successful, remember that true success goes far beyond talent and achievement. It always comes down to who we are as people — our spirit.

That quality then becomes reflected in everything we do and ultimately translates to our success personally and professionally.

YOU CAN'T GIVE MORE THAN YOU RECEIVE

One day my friend Mike Rayburn said in passing, "It's impossible to give more than you receive." I've been quoting him ever since. If we lived by this statement and focused on how much we could give to others, our lives would be rich beyond measure. Ironically, following this spiritual principle is the essence of becoming successful in building material wealth as well!

Happiness is like the air we breathe. We can't see it, we can't buy or sell it, we can't horde it. No one can put it in a box or behind glass. It is, rather, a gift from God to be experienced, to be savored, to be enjoyed.

And sometimes happiness is disguised as sacrifice. Nancy and I have three boys and a little girl. They all depend on us to be good providers and to offer solid leadership. This continual responsibility is sometimes overwhelming, but it's the richest part of my life, the part that brings me the deepest joy. As any parent would agree, the rewards that come from raising a family far outweigh any of the sacrifices involved. By letting go of our self-centered desires to focus on the needs of our family, we begin to discover the secret to happiness. Perhaps we can only attain it by giving it away. Happiness and success will come from the blessings we bring to others.

Remember, happiness is spiritual, not material. Happiness is discovered as we spend our energy giving to others. Happiness is the cultivation of a grateful heart.

The obstacles that hold us back from succeeding
are almost always internal.

Honor, honesty, and integrity are essential ingredients
in cultivating abundance and happiness.

CHAPTER ELEVEN

REMEMBERING THE HIGHER CALLING

There are two kinds of gratitude:
the sudden kind we feel for what we take:
and the larger kind we feel for what we give.

— E. A. Robinson

I n the last chapter I spoke of finding happiness and abundance in our lives. There's almost nothing more important — except one thing: our contribution to others. This is our highest calling, the highest form of success we can achieve. All of us have the privilege and responsibility to reach beyond ourselves and share the blessings and bounty we've been given. The paradoxical truth is that we only really become rich when we enter a life of service. Giving to others is true wealth. We all know that true wealth is not just the accumulation of materials and finances, nor is it power and security. Conversely, it's also not about casting all desire for financial independence aside and taking a vow of poverty.

Although I believe that some of us are called to a life of service free from material distractions, most of us are not. The path of true wealth lies somewhere in the middle. It's a delicate balance. As I said earlier, separating spirituality from the rest of our lives is like shooting ourselves in the foot. Our spiritual path is what fuels us to better our lives. And in our search for ultimate fulfillment we begin to discover that happiness comes from serving others.

WHAT IS OUR HIGHER CALLING?

Perhaps our purpose here on earth is to help one another learn and evolve, bringing us closer to God, closer to each other. By learning to sacrifice we experience wholeness. This mission lasts a lifetime. We must never stop learning how we can help others in meaningful ways. We must never stop uncovering the depth of our relationship with God. This is our Higher Calling.

Have you ever witnessed a child who won't share a soft drink with her parent who just bought it for her? I was recently with someone whose child did just that. The father smiled and said, "She just doesn't get it yet." That's the way it is with us humans. So many people receive incredible blessings and then refuse to share them. They fear someone might take it all back or that there won't be enough. Maybe God is thinking, "They just don't get it yet." The reason that we don't share enough, give enough, help others enough, or love enough is simple — fear. Hey, sorry it's so simple, but it is that simple. It's our human fear of not getting our fair share, of not having enough. It's a mindset of scarcity.

WORLD of ABUNDANCE

Many people simply believe the world is based on survival of the fittest. They think it's about competition — with one person's gain becoming another's loss. For people to take that point of view to its logical conclusion puts us back in the Stone Age. For thousands of years we have been evolving. Now we have the power, the knowledge, and the resources to raise our ideals. It's part of being human — to rise above our base instincts.

But first ask yourself what your beliefs regarding abundance and scarcity are. If you believe we are living in world where there is only so much space, so much food, and only limited resources then you'll always be living in fear of not having enough. If you believe we live in a world of abundance, then your generosity with time, energy, and money will be based on the idea that there is bounty for all. This is not to say that enormous issues concerning our natural resources don't exist. And I'm not suggesting we get into a mind-set of high consumption so we can further indulge ourselves with material pleasures. What I am saying is that with a belief in abundance you'll want to share your rewards with others. It takes courage to give freely. When you believe that God is a God of abundance then you begin to overcome fear and doubt. This leads to a powerful sense of certainty in our lives.

CONTRIBUTING BEYOND OURSELVES

In my first audiotape learning series I talked about making quantum leaps in our lives. I told the story of Philip Hickey, how in less than ten years he went from one restaurant with about seventy-five employees to almost two hundred restaurants with fourteen thousand employees! Well, one of the things that I admire about Phil is the commitment he and his wife, Reedy, have to giving back some of the abundance they've been given. One way they do this is by caring for newborn babies waiting for adoption. They take in babies who are only one or two days old and look after them for up to three months. So far they've taken in twenty-six. If you have children, you know that in that early stage they need loads of attention. They need to be held and monitored constantly. Taking care of these infants is truly a labor of love. Phil and Reedy are remembering their Higher Calling. Their service goes far beyond simply giving money. Building up wealth and then giving it away is a most noble thing to do, but giving of your time is an even greater contribution. Yet Reedy tells me they feel like they're the ones who receive the greatest blessing. That's the miraculous paradox of giving.

> *The great use of life is to spend it for something*
> *that will outlast it.*
>
> — William James

There's nothing more rewarding than helping others. We get a feeling of pure satisfaction, giving us that enthusiasm for life that can be so elusive. The irony is that if everyone contributed, we would not only benefit personally, but we would also solve many of the world's biggest problems. The more we learn to let go and contribute, the more emotional and spiritual treasures we will receive — more than we could have ever imagined.

You will become fulfilled to the degree
that you help others.

Gratitude is the secret to a
spiritually abundant life.

DUST AND DIRT

For more than fifteen years I've been active in the fight against world poverty. This cause has been my passion, my mission, and my quest. Every once in a while a college will bring me to play for a fundraiser to raise awareness about the plight of impoverished children. They know I'll be able to tie my performance in with their efforts. One such school was Arizona Western College. They asked if I could come in for five days and perform at a half dozen high schools in the southern part of the state. The college sponsored the program as an arts outreach to the community, particularly to underprivileged schools. The students who attend these schools are the children of migrant workers, many of whom live in camps set up outside dusty little towns along the Arizona-Mexico border.

The best hope for these students is the chance for an education, a privilege that often goes unappreciated by many Americans. Even though these schools are in the United States, some were as rundown and dilapidated as those in poorer countries. But the students were great! They were enthusiastic and appreciated having someone perform for them.

Try not to become a person of success,
but rather a person of value.

— Albert Einstein

During my five-day stay, I was taken to a little orphanage in the town of San Luis, Mexico, just across the border from Yuma, Arizona. The forty or fifty children living in Bethel Orfanatorio were at the bottom of a crumbling social ladder. They had absolutely nothing. The orphanage had no funding except for donations and volunteer help. As we drove through the streets of San Luis, we saw that the roads, houses, and yards were completely covered with dust. It was a bleak and surreal landscape. I had never seen anything like it, not even in my visit to the poorest parts of Haiti. As we pulled up to the orphanage, the children were sitting around a couple of picnic tables. This was their playground; there was not one blade of grass anywhere, just dust and dirt.

Success has nothing to do with what you gain in life
or accomplish for yourself. It's what you do for others.

— Danny Thomas

Our plan was to find out what food they needed and head off to the local market. But this turned out to be quite a challenge. None of them could speak English, and we couldn't speak Spanish. After a few minutes of gesturing, several of the young women got in our van and pointed the way to the Mexican super-market about ten miles away. It was a bit like those in the States, but many of the essential foods were sold in bulk. Of course, I couldn't read the labels or comprehend the pricing. At first, I suspected these women might take advantage of me by pointing me at the most expensive foods. But nothing could have been further from the truth.

Our first stop was the produce area, and they put a dozen apples into our cart. Then I added four dozen more because, after all, there were forty mouths to feed. We did the same with carrots, potatoes, bananas, and so on. Then we moved on to grains. They scooped five pounds of rice into a bag; I motioned to the clerk to bring us a 50-pound bag from the back room. This went on for about an hour, until one of the girls had tears in her eyes. It was becoming obvious how much the supplies, which we take for granted, were desperately needed.

They were interested only in the absolute essentials. I kept thinking, "Let's get some soda or other fun food for the kids." But they were operating at a survival level I didn't really understand. By the time we had finished, we had seven shopping carts filled to the brim. Between currency and language barriers, it took two hours to get checked out! It really makes you appreciate the speed with which we get things done in the States. At last we loaded up the van and headed back to the orphanage.

It was about 10 P.M. when we returned, and the children had bedded down for the night. When the three older adults watching over things began helping us unload, their gratitude showed in their smiles. This is when reality started setting in for me. As we began bringing the groceries into the small, stark kitchen it hit me — there was no food anywhere. Every cupboard was completely empty.

Did those children go to bed hungry? What would they have had for breakfast? Where would they find food for the next week? That moment is something I think about to this day. People like you and me are presented with opportunities to help others every day. Most of the time the situation isn't quite so intense. It might be as simple as helping the trash collector empty your garbage can into the truck. Or helping the cashier by packing your own grocery bags. Or maybe you *will* be presented with something more dramatic. But the irony is that with every kind word or good deed we offer to others, we become the richer for it. My trip to that orphanage was my proof of this. The smiles on the faces of the orphanage employees were my greatest reward.

I have found the paradox that if I love until it hurts,
then there is no hurt, but only more love.

— Mother Teresa

Once the groceries had been unpacked, the two young Mexican women led me to a series of cinderblock rooms with cots lined up along the walls. There they were, all forty children sound asleep. Some were as young as three and four. They huddled together two and three to a bed. It was cold, perhaps forty-five degrees, and half of them had no blankets. The sight tore my heart out. As the father of four, I can deeply appreciate how important it is for children to be touched and held. I can hardly imagine how children survive without nurturing parents to comfort them. These children had no one to hold them while they fell asleep or when they woke up crying after a bad dream. It was overwhelming.

Late that night, as I headed back to my warm, comfortable hotel room in Yuma, my heart was pounding with conflicting emotions. I felt embarrassed. How could I ever complain about anything again? How could I return to my luxurious and comfortable home and ignore this need? What could I do to make a difference? I knew I had just had one of the richest experiences life has to offer. I've raised hundreds of thousands of dollars for the poor from the concert stage. I've spent a week traveling through Haiti seeing the poorest of the poor firsthand. But only when I became personally invested and experienced these children's plight could I feel their pain. Mother Teresa described their plight as the "face of poverty." As we take charge of our lives, let us think beyond the pursuit of achievement and acquisitions — to discovering our Higher Calling.

> *Many persons have a wrong idea*
> *of what constitutes true happiness.*
> *It is not attained through self-gratification,*
> *but through fidelity to a worthy purpose.*
>
> **— Helen Keller**

When we slow down and take stock of our lives, there can be no doubt that God has blessed us beyond measure. With encouragement, almost any child can achieve extraordinary things. If you are reading this book, I am going to assume that you have much for which to be grateful. Those who have been given more have the privilege and the responsibility to be good stewards of those blessings. We all know that when we reach out and give of ourselves, we receive the richest blessing of all: a sense of meaning and purpose during our stay in this world.

Let's never forget that the human spirit is inherently generous. That generosity will be reflected in our compassion for and service to others. It's how we will find our Higher Calling. It's how we will find a truly abundant life.

Cultivating gratitude is a skill that can be learned.

Finding the meaning of life starts with investing
the gifts God has given us.

Throughout this book I've spent much time talking about overcoming self-imposed limitations. I've encouraged you to dream big, to plan carefully, and then to take some risks. Most important, I encourage you to stay focused on who you are as a person, to stay true to your Higher Calling. That's a wonderful plan for life! I hope my stories have shown that it's all possible — because it is! So dare to embrace each day with great anticipation. Don't be afraid of adversity. It will strengthen you. Don't be afraid of the unknown, for in it lie the secrets of the universe. Learn from every new experience and then move forward. Look for the good in everyone you meet. Think about what success means to you. Think about all the abundance that's in your life already.

The degree to which we live by the principles I've shared in this book will be the degree of our happiness and fulfillment. Of course, I personally struggle with the challenges, setbacks, and hardships I've talked about — just as you will struggle with yours. (Just ask my children. Just ask my wife!) But I always remember that it's a good, noble, and worthwhile struggle. Thank you for joining me on this quest for an excellent life. I hope our paths cross again soon.

BIBLIOGRAPHY

Abraham, Jay. *Money-Making Secrets of Marketing Genius Jay Abraham.* Rolling Hills Estates, Calif.: Abraham Publishing Group, Inc., 1993.

Allen, James. *As a Man Thinketh.* New York: Putnam Publishing Group, 1959.

Andrews, Andy. *Storms of Perfection: In Their Own Words.* Nashville, Tenn.: Lightning Crown Publishers, 1991.

Armstrong, Lance. *It's Not about the Bike: My Journey Back to Life.* New York: The Berkley Publishing Group, 2001.

Blanchard, Ken and Brian Tracy. *How Leaders LEAD: The Essential Skills for Career and Personal Success.* Chicago: Dartnell, 1989.

Blechman, Bruce and Jay Conrad Levinson. *Guerrilla Financing: Alternative Techniques to Finance Any Small Business.* Boston: Houghton Mifflin Company, 1991.

Brown, Les. *The Power of Purpose: How to Create the Life You Always Wanted.* Niles, Ill.: Nightingale-Conant Corporation, 1998.

Covey, Stephen R. *First Things First: To Life, to Love, to Learn, to Leave a Legacy.* New York: Simon & Schuster, 1994.

_____. *The Seven Habits of Highly Effective People: Restoring the Character Ethic.* New York: Simon & Schuster, 1989.

Dell, Michael. *Direct from Dell: Strategies That Revolutionized an Industry.* New York: HarperCollins, 1999.

Dent, Harvey S., Jr. *The Roaring 2000s: Building the Wealth and Lifestyle You Desire in the Greatest Boom in History.* New York: Simon & Schuster, 1998.

Drucker, Peter F. *The Effective Executive.* New York: HarperPaperbacks, 1993.

Dyer, Wayne W. *You'll See It When You Believe It: The Way to Your Personal Transformation.* New York: Avon Books, 1989.

_____. *Your Erroneous Zones.* New York: HarperPaperbacks, 1993.

_____. *Your Sacred Self: Making the Decision to Be Free.* New York: HarperPaperbacks, 1995.

Fuller, R. Buckminster. *Intuition.* New York: Anchor Books, 1973.

Gegax, Tom. *Winning in the Game of Life: Self-Coaching Secrets for Success.* New York: Three Rivers Press, 1999.

Greene, Bob and Oprah Winfrey. *Make the Connection: Ten Steps to a Better Body—and a Better Life.* New York: Hyperion, 1996.

Greene, Robert. *The 48 Laws of Power.* New York: Viking Penguin, 1998.

Hill, Napoleon. *Think and Grow Rich.* Niles, Ill.: Nightingale-Conant Corporation, 1993.

Iacocca, Lee. *Iacocca: An Autobiography.* New York: Bantam Books, 1984.

Judd, Naomi. *Love Can Build a Bridge.* New York: Random House, 1993.

_____. *Personal Victory: Building the Life You Love in 21 Days.* Naomi Judd Inc., 1998.

Kersey, Cynthia. *Unstoppable: 45 Powerful Stories of Perseverance and Triumph from People Just Like You.* Naperville, Ill.: Sourcebooks, Inc., 1998.

Lee, Blaine. *The Power Principle: Influence with Honor.* New York: Simon & Schuster, 1997.

Mackay, Harvey. *How to Build a Network of Power Relationships.* Niles, Ill.: Nightingale-Conant, 1995.

_____. *Pushing the Envelope: All the Way to the Top.* New York: Ballantine, 1999.

_____. *Swim with the Sharks without Being Eaten Alive: Outsell, Outmanage, Outmotivate, and Outnegotiate Your Competition.* New York: William Morrow and Company, Inc., 1988.

Mandino, Og. *The Greatest Salesman in the World.* New York: Bantam, 1968.

McCormack, Mark H. *On Managing.* West Hollywood, Calif.: Dove Books, 1996.

_____. *What They Don't Teach You at Harvard Business School.* New York: Bantam Doubleday Dell Publishers, 1988.

Moore, Gary D. *Ten Golden Rules for Financial Success.* Grand Rapids, Mich.: Zondervan Publishing House, 1996.

Nightingale, Earl. *On Success.* Niles, Ill.: Nightingale-Conant Corporation, 1988.

Orman, Suze. *The 9 Steps to Financial Freedom: Practical & Spiritual Steps So You Can Stop Worrying.* New York: Crown Publishers, Inc., 1997.

Peale, Norman Vincent. *The Power of Positive Thinking.* Pawling, N.Y.: Peale Foundation, Inc., 1995.

Pilzer, Paul Zane. *Unlimited Wealth: The Theory and Practice of Economic Alchemy.* New York: Crown Publishers, Inc., 1990.

Redstone, Sumner. *A Passion to Win.* New York: Simon & Schuster, 2001.

Ries, Al. *Focus: The Future of Your Company Depends on It.* New York: HarperCollins, 1996.

BIBLIOGRAPHY

Ries, Al and Jack Trout. *Positioning: The Battle for Your Mind.* New York: Warner Books, 1981.

_____. *The 22 Immutable Laws of Marketing.* New York: HarperBusiness, 1993.

Robbins, Anthony. *Awaken the Giant Within: How to Take Immediate Control of Your Mental, Emotional, Physical and Financial Destiny.* New York: Simon & Schuster, 1991.

_____. *Lessons in Mastery.* Niles, Ill.: Nightingale-Conant Corporation, 1998.

_____. *Living Health.* Niles, Illinois: Nightingale-Conant Corporation, 1991.

_____. *Personal Power II: The Driving Force.* San Diego: Robbins Research International, Inc., 1996.

_____. *PowerTalk Audio Magazine: Strategies for Lifelong Success.* San Diego: Robbins Research International, Inc., 1993.

_____. *Unleash the Power Within: Personal Coaching to Transform Your Life!* Niles, Ill.: Nightingale-Conant Corporation, 1999.

_____. *Unlimited Power.* New York: Fawcett Columbine, 1986.

_____. *Unlimited Power: Home Study Course.* San Diego: Robbins Research International, Inc., 1991.

Schor, Juliet B. *The Overspent American: Upscaling, Downshifting, and the New Consumer.* New York: Basic Books, 1998.

Slater, Robert. *Jack Welch and the GE Way: Management Insights and Leadership Secrets of the Legendary CEO.* New York: McGraw-Hill, 1999.

Stanley, Thomas J. *The Millionaire Mind.* Kansas City, Mo.: Andrews McMeel Publishing, 2000.

Stanley, Thomas J. and William D. Danko. *The Millionaire Next Door: The Surprising Secrets of America's Wealthy.* Atlanta: Longstreet Press, Inc., 1996.

Stovall, Jim. *You Don't Have to Be Blind to See.* Nashville: Thomas Nelson, Inc., Publishers, 1996.

Templeton, John Marks. *Laws of Inner Wealth: Principles for Spiritual and Material Abundance.* Niles, Ill.: Nightingale-Conant Corporation, 1997.

_____. *Worldwide Laws of Life: 200 Eternal Spiritual Principles.* Philadelphia: Templeton Foundation Press, 1997.

Tracy, Brian. *Breaking the Success Barrier: Using Strategic Thinking Skills to Accelerate Your Goals.* Niles, Ill.: Nightingale-Conant Corporation, 1998.

_____. *How to Master Your Time: The Special Art of Increasing Your Productivity.* Niles, Ill.: Nightingale-Conant Corporation, 1989.

_____. *Maximum Achievement: Strategies and Skills That Will Unlock Your Hidden Powers to Succeed.* New York: Fireside, 1993.

_____. *Million Dollar Habits: 12 Power Practices to DOUBLE and TRIPLE your Income.* Niles, Ill.: Nightingale-Conant Corporation, 1999.

_____. *The Luck Factor: How to Take the Chance Out of Becoming a Success.* Niles, Illinois: Nightingale-Conant Corporation, 1997.

_____. *The 100 Absolutely Unbreakable Laws of Business Success.* San Francisco: Berrett-Koehler Publishers, Inc., 2000.

_____. *The Psychology of Achievement.* Niles, Ill.: Nightingale-Conant Corporation, 1984.

_____. *The Science of Self-Confidence.* Niles, Ill.: Nightingale-Conant Corporation, 1991.

_____. *Thinking Big: The Keys to Personal Power and Maximum Performance.* Niles, Ill.: Nightingale-Conant Corporation, 1996.

Waitley, Denis. *The Seven Sacred Truths.* Niles, Ill.: Nightingale-Conant Corporation, 2000.

Walton, Sam. *Made in America: My Story.* New York: Doubleday, 1992.

Ziglar, Zig. *Top Performance: How to Develop Excellence in Yourself and Others.* Niles, Ill.: Nightingale-Conant Corporation, 1989.

ABOUT THE AUTHOR

R obin is an author, motivational speaker, entrepreneur, and one of the world's most innovative guitarists. Robin is the owner of Dark Horse Recording, a magical recording studio complex on his horse farm just outside Nashville, Tennessee, where he lives with his wife and four children. Starting with only $2,000, Robin built Dark Horse into a multi-million-dollar recording facility that has attracted some of the biggest recording artists in the world. Jewel, Amy Grant, Faith Hill, Neil Diamond, Michael McDonald, Dolly Parton, and Alison Krauss are just a few of the artists who have come to Dark Horse to record.

In addition to his business success, Robin has also forged an extraordinary career as a guitarist, releasing nine albums, performing more than two thousand concerts, and appearing on dozens of television shows. *The Boston Post Gazette* wrote, "Crow is a guitar genius!" and the *Florida Times Union* says, "Crow's music is a rocket launcher for the imagination." He has toured in support of such bands as Cheap Trick, Peter Frampton, Spyro Gyra, and others.

In 1996 Robin received the Harry Chapin Humanitarian Award for his work in fighting poverty and hunger in the developing world. Currently, he tours arenas and convention centers nationwide, offering a unique blend of motivational speaking and guitar performance. For more information see his websites: www.robincrow.com and www.darkhorserecording.com.